WHY RESERVATION FOR MUSLIMS?

WHY RESERVATION FOR MUSLIMS?

Habibur Rehman

GYAN

Why Reservation for Muslims?

ISBN : 978-81-212-1155-0

Published in 2013 in India by
Gyan Publishing House
23, Main Ansari Road, Daryaganj,
New Delhi - 110002
Phones : 23282060, 23261060
Fax : (011) 23285914
E-mail: books@gyanbooks.com
website: gyanbooks.com

Laser Type Setting : Rajender Vashist, Delhi
Printed at : Chawla Offset Printers, Delhi

Contents

Preface

There is a wide range of variations in the conditions of Muslims across the country, but one thing is certain that Muslims as a whole exhibit the perceived discrimination and deprivation practically in every segment of the country. There is vast development deficit together with the feeling of extreme neglect which has disheartened the largest minority of the country. Apart from having the identity and security crises, they are also facing several issues pertaining to equity, equality and justice both at macro and micro levels. Muslims of India have become virtually a distinct identity because of their depleted social and cultural frame of reference. Most of them can be spotted easily with frustration lit large on their foreheads, despondency peeping from their piercing eyes and depression reflecting from their conversations. They are on the lowest pedestal of the society and they need affirmative actions to bring them within the national milieu failing which they would be pushed to the ghettos to become a new class of dalits to fill the vacuum created by the upward movement of SCs/STs and Backward Classes. The Sachar Committee Report and the Misra Commission findings too have revealed that Muslims are economically, educationally, socially and culturally a miserable lot. In many respects they are worse than Scheduled Castes and Scheduled Tribes. They are under siege due to lack of education, shrinking political space, deprivation and frustration. There is a strong feeling amongst them that many a time they face constant fear, insecurity and humiliation. They claim that their participation in industry, trade and commerce is nil, their representation in government jobs is minimal and they are conspicuous by absence in the private sector. The governing structure claims that a wide variety of policies and programmes were undertaken for the amelioration of Muslims but the general impression among Muslims is that these were not enough since the development deficit between them and others is widening day by day.

It is certain that all the allegations and perceptions of Muslims may not be true but they have not been built on the basis of hunches. Some of their charges of unfair treatment may have genuine contents of truth which support their contentions and enable them to air their grievances from time to time. In a situation like this the ceaseless recrimination and mutual accusation result in heart burning and war of attrition and distrust. Efforts should be made to find the solution to the complex problem before it that it begins to cause dent within the composite and pluralistic fabric of the nation. Attempts should also be made on priority basis by the state machinery to develop an effective mechanism supported by well-guarded legal system so that the complaints of discrimination and the grievances of the depressed groups may be addressed expeditiously. Without going into fault finding, it is in the national interest as well as in the interest of Muslims that they should be treated as a depressed, marginalized and backward section of the society *en mass* and steps should be taken to uplift them through affirmative and positive welfare measures. Without this it is next to impossible for them to come out of the vicious circle of poverty and development.

There is a sense of despair among Muslims after having seen the knee-jerk reaction of the Government in matters of implementation of the Sachar Committee Report. They are tired of election time promises and presenting memorandums after memorandums to the government without any results. They want quick, bold and fruitful result to their vexed problems. Misra Commission has done a yeoman service to Muslims by analyzing their social, educational and economic problems thread bare. It has suggested welfare measures for the development of weaker sections of Muslims including reservation in educational institutions and government jobs on the pattern of SCs/STs and Backward Classes. It has also chalked out the modalities for the implementation of its recommendations within the framework of Indian Constitution. A serious debate is going on in the country and most of the

Muslims including the intellectuals, clergies, professionals, technocrats, bureaucrats and commoners are in favour of reservation. However, it is irony of fate that the ghost of separate electorate of pre-partition days is looming so large on the political horizon of the country that no political party appears willing to concede reservation to Muslims despite having seen the well proven and well articulated decadence of Muslims. It is a golden opportunity for the Government to salvage the long pending problem of Muslims. Since the Government had instituted the Commission, it is hoped that it would earnestly implement the recommendations of the Commission and rescue Muslims from constant fears and frustrations.

I am thankful to Justice Sachar and his colleagues for submitting a comprehensive report on "Social, Economic and Educational Status of the Muslim Community" and Justice Ranganath Misra and the members of National Commission for Religious and Linguistic Minorities Commission for suggesting welfare measures for marginalized sections of Muslims which helped me to give a shape to this venture.

I also feels grateful to my wife Mrs. Masarrat Habib, daughter Dr. Sitwat Khan, son Eng. Bilal Habib, son-in-law Dr. Jamshedur Rehman Khan, grand son-in law Dr. Danish Kazmi, daughter-in-law Dr. Reshma Mukhtar, grandson Master Basil Habib Khan, and grand daughters Dr. Areeba Kazmi Khan, Eng. Abeer Khan, Ms Rahma Habib Khan and Ms Rifa Habib Khan and all other well wishers whose help, assistance and cooperation helped me t7o give a plausible shape to this work.

Habibur Rehman

1

Ramifications of being a Minority in India

Indian Constitution provides several safeguards for the protection, equity, equality, safety, amelioration and uplift of minorities. The planning process in the country too has contributed in the economic empowerment, enrichment and the betterment of the standard of living of people. Still the perception among Muslims is that they have been left alone in the process of growth and development. They feel that not only the deprivation is widespread but they are also lagging behind in most of the human development indicators. Besides, the economic, educational and social gap between them and the rest of the communities is widening day by day. It was observed that since there was lack of authentic information about the social, economic and educational status of Muslims in India, many vested interests took the advantage of this lacuna and attributed several labels against Muslims including the appeasement. In the absence of any systematic analysis and availability of reliable data, the debate centered around perceptions and rhetoric. The Government of India too could not adopt any specific affirmative policies and programmes to address the issues relating to Muslims and other religious and linguistic minorities. However, with the publication of Sachar Committee Report, when it became clear that the Muslim community exhibited deficits and deprivation practically in all dimensions, the Muslims, the Central and State Governments and the civil society became active. Consequently, the National Commission for Religious and

Linguistic Minorities was constituted to suggest measures and in its Report the Commission has recommended various schemes including reservation for Muslims in educational institutions and government jobs. In this study we are trying to analyze the ground realities pertaining to the social, economic and political conditions of Muslims vis-à-vis other segments of the society with a view to perceive the logic and justification behind the various measures including reservations suggested by the Commission for the Religious and Linguistic Minorities.

It has been noted that the sense of insecurity, the crisis of identity, the lack of equity and the question of non-inclusion in the process of development as well as the lack of space in governing structure has made many Muslims to perceive these problems as community-specific though there are diversity of views within the community about the prevalence and severities of these issues. Just as there is diversity in perceiving these problems, views about how they could be addressed are also diverse. There is a widespread demand for positive, affirmative and proactive action by the Government including reservation and separate quota in educational institutions, Government jobs and legislative bodies to up lift Muslims from the morass. It is felt by many that to bring Muslims at par with other segments of the society, reservation on the pattern of Scheduled Castes, Scheduled Tribes and Backward Classes is the only solution to take them out of the vicious circle of backwardness and poverty. Those who support reservation include such segments also who stress that the facility of reservation should be provided only to dalit or extremely backward Muslims, while others maintain that the facility should be provided to the entire community since almost all the Muslims in the country are miserably backward. There is no dearth of people who want reservation on economic basis and there are many who insist that instead of religion-based quota the access to education and employment must be sought through OBC quota or good educational facilities under the non-discriminatory atmosphere. Those who oppose reservation claim that reservation would kill the initiative and dynamism among Muslim youths and make them docile and dependent and have negative repercussions. There is near unanimity among Muslims that Scheduled Castes among Muslims should be given all those benefits that are given to Hindu Scheduled Castes. There is also general consensus in the community that Muslims should take the maximum use of the prevailing caste categories for quotas as they are not only constitutionally tenable but have also acquired respectability. Besides, there is also a widespread agreement among Muslim masses that so long as reservation is being used as the instrument to uplift any community in the country, Muslims too being educationally and economically backward, should seek reservation through Constitutional means as the Article 46 of the Directive Principle of State Policy in the Constitution mandates the State to promote educational and economic interests of the weaker sections of people.

It is an open secret that the demand for reservation for Muslims has acquired an added strength after the publication of Justice Ranganath Misra Report. Indian Muslims have been demanding reservation since the installation of the Constitution in the country in educational institutions and government jobs as well as in legislative bodies from Parliament to Panchayats on the pattern of reservation provided to the SCs/STs because they feel that they are not only socially, politically, educationally and economically at par with the dalits but have also been left helpless after the Partition of the country. However, in the context of the bitter experience of the partition of the country on communal lines, their demand for reservation at the time of framing the Indian constitution was not acceded by the Constituent Assembly because many people expressed their fears that the reservation for Muslims would go against the national interest. Muslims became silent for the conditions prevailing in those days were not favorable to them due to creation of Partition on the basis of "Two- Nation Theory". In the later period also nobody came in support of reservation in favour of Muslims. Moreover, several rightist Parties and extremist organizations had propounded artificial theory of "Appeasement of Muslims" so artfully repeating it thousand times in such a manner that people had begun to believe that Muslims needed no special treatment as they were already better off and the most privileged part of the society due to their vote bank politics and most favourable treatment provided to them by the Congress Government to garner their bulk votes. Thanks to the Sachar Committee Report that it falsified the theory of appeasement and the people realized that the bogy of "Appeasement of Muslims" was merely a ploy to keep them permanently under the debris. As a matter of fact, Muslims in almost all the segments of Indian economy were behind all sections of the society including Higher Castes, Backward Castes and other minorities. In many respects they were even below Scheduled Castes and Scheduled Tribes. The stark realities awakened them from their dogmatic slumber. After having known the real facts about their decadence when they realized that they were not only backward but the economic and educational gap between them and the rest was widening, they came on the road and demanded reservation. The political parties and the ruling governments too came on the defensive. Some of the Congress ruled and non-Congress-ruled States provided marginal reservations to educationally, socially and economically backward sections of Muslims under the backward category. The Karnataka Government provided a paltry reservation to entire lot of Muslims considering them *en mass* as educationally, socially and economically backward. There are several States which are thinking in terms of providing reservations to depressed class of Muslims within the category of the Backward Castes.

National Commission for Minorities

The issue of reservation for Muslims got stimulus after the Sachar Committee findings. A debate started in the country about the desirability of providing reservation to Muslims. There was no dearth of people who emphasized that Muslims could not be provided reservation purely on the basis of religion as per the spirit of the Indian Constitution. Others claimed that they could be provided reservation being the marginalized, less privileged and depressed sections under the category of Backward Castes subject to the overall 50% limit. Many rightist political parties tried to put the issue of reservation of Muslims under the carpet by playing vote bank politics and many parties went to the law courts including the High Courts and Supreme Court which created a national debate and generated heat in the country. Consequently, to arrive at some meaningful solution the Government of India resolved to constitute a

National Commission for Religious and Linguistic Minorities on 29th October, 2004 consisting of three members under the Chairmanship of Justice Ranganath Misra.

The terms of reference included:

(a) To suggest criteria for identification of socially and economically backward sections among religious and linguistic minorities;

(b) To recommend measures for welfare of socially and economically backward sections among religious and linguistic minorities, including reservation in education and government employment;

(c) To suggest the necessary constitutional, legal and administrative modalities required for the implementation of its recommendations.

After nearly five months of its hard work, the Commissions' Terms of Reference were modified so as to add the following to its original Terms of Reference:

To give its recommendations on the issues raised in WPs 180/04 and 94/05 in the Supreme Court and in certain High Courts relating to Para 3 of the Constitution (Scheduled Castes) Order 1950 in the context of ceiling of 50 per cent on reservations as also the modalities of inclusion in the list of Scheduled Castes. The tenure of the Commission was periodically extended up to 15th May, 2007 and the Commission finally submitted its report in two comprehensive Volumes on 10th May, 2007.

The Commission extensively studied the Constitutional and Legislative Provisions regarding minorities and thoroughly analyzed the status of the Religious and Linguistic Minorities as well as the status of women among Minorities. It suggested certain criteria for identifying backward sections among Religious Minorities and also recommended measures for welfare and development of minorities including reservation as a welfare measure. The Commission also studied the demands for amending Constitution (SC) Order, 1950 and finally ended with recommendations and modalities for implementation.

The Commission emphasized that the Minorities were an

integral part of every nation. They existed in every country and almost all the civilized nations were committed to the equality of citizens without any kind of discrimination and the national states were duty bound to preserve, protect and assure the rights of minorities in matters of religion, culture, belief system, language and traditions. The promotion and protection of the rights of people belonging to minorities contribute to the political and social stability as well as peace and development of every country. Meeting the aspirations of the minorities and ensuring their rights, acknowledging the dignity and equality of all individuals in a participatory and inclusive development process within the harmonious and pluralistic framework, strengthens the faith and confidence of minorities. The Commission felt that there was a concealed dichotomy among the majorities and the minorities. The majorities mostly perceive the minorities as others and there is an implied tendency among them to assimilate the minorities within their national frameworks. As against this, the minorities always fear the perceived domination by the majorities and try to insulate them against the onslaught of their big brothers with a view to protect their individualities, identities and religious and cultural distinctiveness. Thus, the UN Declaration on the Rights of Minorities 1992 enjoins the States to protect the existence, honour and possessions of minorities within their respective territories and asks them to create conditions for promotion of their identity, self-respect and dignity, It also mandates them to ensure that persons belonging to minorities not only effectively exercise human rights and fundamental freedoms with full equality and without any discrimination but also develop their culture, language, religion, traditions and customs. Finally, it emphasizes on effectively planning and implementation of national policy and programmes with due regard to the legitimate interest of minorities.

Peculiarities of Various Minorites

Though the demography of minorities, their sex composition, literacy and educational status, marital position, livelihood pattern, rural urban distribution, type of landholdings, source of income and health indicators show their quality of life to some extent but they seldom reflect their social customs, cultural niceties', moral perceptions, religious conventions and distinguishing and salient features. In modern times the liberalization and globalization are rapidly transforming the socio-economic structures of minorities and majorities. Besides, the diversification of economic pursuits, urbanization, westernization of education, adoption of western ways of living and inter-caste marriages are converging the apparent differences between the minorities and the majorities. The time is not too far when they would resemble with each other in many ways as water resembles with water. Jews despite being a minority are an integral part of United States of America and many European countries. Likewise, Christians too being an important minority are the vital parts of many countries in Asia and Africa. Both these significant minorities resemble with others in matters of sex ratio, age at marriages, infant and child mortality rate, nutritional status, use of contraceptives, fertility and mortality rates, literacy level, educational status, rural urban pattern, average house-hold size, ownership of houses, average income, dependency ratio, work participation rate, etc. Still they are treated as minorities because they differ in several ways in their faith, belief system and religious connotations. Minorities being religious or ethnic groups with distinct social and cultural pattern are demarcated from other segments of the society primarily due to their religion or language. They cannot be identified merely by their socio-economic status, politico-cultural and demographic criteria though many a time their salient features are reflected by such criteria. If we look at Indian minorities, we find that Parsis, Christians, Sikhs and Jains are far better compared to the majority community in various economic, social, political, cultural, health care and other parameters yet they are known as minorities. Sikhs are mostly recognized by their hair and turban and for their zeal in religion. Likewise, the Parsis are known for their exclusive and distinct life style and not by any demographic or socio-economic criteria. Similarly, Jains despite being a minority are hardly distinguished from rest of the majority community save on their religious ceremonies.

As far as Muslims are concerned, they too are a minority in the context of vast Hindu Majority though in absolute terms they are numerically superior to many European countries. As a distinct religious community they are recognized by their absolute belief in one and only One supreme God, unparallel respect for Holy Quran and un alloyed obedience to the Holy Prophet. They are marked by their prayers five times a day and fasting in the month of Ramadan and their Eid festivities as well as their zeal with which they pay Zakat and go to perform Hajj. Their ladies with faces covered, elders with their graceful beards, children reciting the verses of Holy Quran distinguish them from others. Their skull caps, towering Sherwanis, marks of prostration on their foreheads, pious Nikah ceremonies and the graceful burial of their dead provide them distinct identity. Their concept of Halal and Haram or Permissible and Non-Permissible, their abhorrence for liquor, gambling and games of chance and their conservative life style provide colour to their distinctiveness. Their sacrificing at the time of Eid-ul-Azha, their mourning during Moharram, their concept of equality in the rows of the mosques and their bowing after their Imams towards Kabah bestow upon them uniqueness. Their delicacies of Urdu ascent, sophisticated etiquettes, reverence for guests and concern for the wayfarers speak volumes of their Muslim identity. Their towering minarets, Azan of the Moazzin, pious shrines, religious Madarsas, historical past and belief system provide them exclusiveness. Their old *maqbaras*, spread out grave yards and birth and death ceremonies mark them from rest of the segments of the society.

Many researchers and social scientists also identify poor and depressed class of Muslims by their economic deprivation, social isolation, moral frustration and political marginalization. Marks of miseries engraved on their dejected faces, gloom overshadowing their skeleton structures and depression reflecting from their gestures and postures pinpoint them. The depleted houses, unhealthy surrounding, illiterate masses and dirty roads and filthy atmosphere lead us towards them. The sense of otherness, lack of space in governing structure and perception of being discriminated signify their presence. Many of them can be easily recognized by being below poverty line, several of them can be spotted toiling as landless labourers and the multitude can be located while moving in search of livelihood. Unemployment, lack of technical skill, low wages and uncertain future are the characteristics of these unfortunate people. It is these people who find it difficult to get houses on rent in majority areas, their children find the doors of good educational institutions half closed due to suspicion and some of them are picked up on slightest doubt by the security agencies. It is these segments of the society who find few friends in the mainstream political parties and civil society. Despite India shining, they are living within the growth-shadow areas and the development gap between them and others is widening day by day making them poorer and poorer. In almost all the sectors of national reconstruction they are behind Hindu Upper Castes, OBCs and other minorities. In several sectors they have fallen behind the Scheduled Castes and Scheduled Tribes. The most unfortunate aspect of this lot of people is that they do not find light at the other end of the tunnel and they are more or less convinced that there are no signs that the philosopher's stone will cause all the pieces to fall neatly into place.

Moreover, there are others who can be observed toiling as mechanics, petty shopkeepers, transport operators, hawkers, Rikshaw Pullers and self-employed agents. Their children can be gazed working as domestic servants to supplement family income, their womenfolk can be seen engaged in household and sub-contracting jobs and their elders can be noticed as burden upon the family. They are conspicuous by absence in Government sector, their number in industry, trade and commerce is minimal and they own no property of any significance. They have maximum number of illiterates, larger number of poor and greater portion of unemployed. It is not difficult to identify them on the basis of their material development for they have benefitted the least from various government policies and programmes mainly due to bias towards them at grass root level and partly due to lack of information and to some extent due to their own lethargy and inferiority complex. Muslims are certainly the prominent part of the composite culture of India and they are as much Indian as others are and their contribution is equally significant as a community of significance in the process of national reconstruction. Several studies undertaken by various government agencies and private organizations have revealed that Muslims of India are economically, socially and educationally miserable lot and they need affirmative actions on the part of the Government and the civil society to bring them out of the vicious circle of poverty and backwardness.

Criteria for Identifying Backward Sections Among Religious Minorities

It is a fact that in a country like India with multi-religious, multi-culture and multi-racial and multi-lingual aspects, it is difficult to identify the socially, educationally and economically backward sections of society because political and vested interests usually make the task difficult. Various parameters were adopted to identify Scheduled Castes, Scheduled Tribes and Backward Castes. The Second Backward Classes Commission 1979, headed by B.P. Mandal suggested 11 criteria. Out of the 11 criteria the Commission recommended four social criteria such as classes considered as socially backward by others, classes/castes which mainly depended upon manual labour for their livelihood, classes where at least 25% females and 10% males above the State average got married at an average of below 17 years in rural areas and 10% females and 5% males do so in urban areas and classes where participation of females in workforce was at least 25% above State average. The three educational parameters included- classes where 25% children above State average in age group of 5-15 years never attended schools, the castes where the rate of student drop out in the age group of 5-15 years was at least 25% above State average and the castes/classes where the proportion of matriculation was at least 25% below the State average. Similarly, the four economic criteria were: castes/classes where the average value of family assets were 25% below state average, the families living in kaccha houses was 25% below national average, where sources of drinking water were beyond half a kilometer for more than 50% households and where the number of households having taken consumption loan was at least 25% above State average. Several experts adopted the 13 parameters such as land, house, clothing, food security, sanitation, consumer durables, literacy, labour force, means of livelihood, status of children, indebtedness, migration and preference for assistance. Others relied upon low social position in the caste-based hierarchal Hindu society, lack of comparatively lower ranking in educational advancement, inadequate representation in Government Services and low participation in industry, trade and commerce. Many took into consideration social factors such as the castes and communities usually considered as socially backward and castes and communities which mainly depended on agriculture or other manual labour for their livelihood and lacked significant resources. For educational backwardness they emphasized castes and communities whose literacy, proportion of Matriculation and proportion of Graduation was at least 8% and 20% less than District and State averages respectively. For economic criteria they stressed castes and communities, a significant number of which lived in Kaccha houses or the share of those members who surrendered agricultural land under Agricultural Ceiling Act of the State was nil or their share in Government Services was not commensurate to their population ratio. There were a few who took into consideration social factors such as the status of the caste/class in the eyes of others, their dependence mainly upon agriculture and manual labour, low marriageable age, greater participation of women in work force, participation of children in work force to supplement family income, association with hereditary and traditional professions, nomadic or semi-nomadic nature of the classes and poor representation in governing structure. Similarly, they took educational criteria such as lower literacy rate than average, lowest proportion of matriculates and others compared to the average and first generation people joining educational stream. Likewise, among economic criteria, extreme poverty, absence of landholding, engagement in agriculture, residence in kaccha houses, lack of infrastructural facilities, indebtedness, migration and less use of consumer durables were taken into consideration while identifying backward classes.

There are many who claim that the existing criteria based on castes, classes, tribes and social, educational and economic backwardness are not satisfactory. The SC/ST/OBC lists have been finalized without any scientific basis since no data-base surveys were undertaken, no identifiable and objective criteria were selected and the emphasis mainly had been on subjective and political considerations rather than on empirical and logical ones. Besides, there is no record in the district office concerning educational status and income levels of families, infrastructural facilities and socio-economic conditions of people below poverty level. Mostly the political considerations have been responsible for the inclusion of various castes in the list of reserved categories. Non-exclusion of ineligible classes has dented the marginalized and backward sections of the society including the minorities among the people at the bottom of the pyramid. Consequently dissensions are growing among various communities since the poorest among the reserved categories have benefitted the least and the creamy layers are usurping their rights. They also held that poverty was not taken into consideration but religion or caste was the basis to identify people. There was near consensus among the meaningful people that religion or castes did not determine socio-economic backwardness. They believe that castes and classes are not homogeneous groups as they include both backward and forward sections. They, therefore, emphasize that family should be considered as the unit and family-wise data should be compiled and the families which have least number of educated girls or which do not have any member with the level of high school should be declared as educationally backward. Likewise, social and economic backwardness too should be assessed by the quantifiable and identifiable social and economic considerations of the families rather than caste or class or religious groups.

There are people who claim that keeping family as the unit of measurement amounts to negation of the whole exercise which was undertaken by the framers of the Constitution for the amelioration of the condition of the handicapped sections of the society. It amounts to saying that reservation should not be provided to Scheduled Castes, Scheduled Tribes and Backward Castes and Minorities on the basis of their weak positions but it should be provided to every segment of socially, educationally and economically backward family irrespective of the fact whether it belongs to the forward and upper castes or poor and marginalized sections of the society. In the opinion of many, this is an intelligent ploy to do away with reservation exclusively to the marginalized sections and provide indirectly reservation to the poor and backward sections from among the already privileged and dominant sections of the society.

Mostly it is claimed that castes and classes should surely and certainly be the basis of reservation for these segments of the society have been exploited over a long period of time merely on the basis of castes and classes. In the same way, religion too should be the basis of reservation especially for Muslims because Indian Muslims after Partition could not take the benefit of various social, educational and economic programmes due to the fact that the blame of Partition was wholly and solely placed on their shoulders as a homogeneous religious community and there was a religious bias against them being Muslims. As against this, the Sikhs, Jains, Parsis and to some extent Christians were not primarily discriminated on the basis of religion in matters of economic, social and educational privileges. Many Muslims claim that even today, there are a few political parties or segments of society who are willing to provide reservation to Muslims on the basis of being Muslims though these sections have no objection if reservation is being given to any Hindu from among the majority community being a Hindu woman, Hindu SC/ST, Hindu OBC or Hindu higher caste. It is a fact that Muslims have not benefitted from economic, social, educational and other developmental programmes. They are especially lacking in the field of education, communication, health, infrastructure and income generation. They are the people at the bottom of Indian society and have remained isolated even after nearly six decades of Independence. Since they are an integral part of the egalitarian Indian society, it is obligatory on the part of the State to take positive and affirmative steps to lift them to a position from where they may take advantages on the equal footings. The Justice Sachar Committee Report and National Commission for Religious and Linguistic Minorities headed by Justice Ranganath Misra also reveal that Indian Muslims are not at par with other segments of Indian society. Being unequal they cannot compete with those who are superior to them. Admittedly, there can be equality only between equals and not between the superiors and handicapped. Equality of opportunity and equality of treatment or treating unequal as equals basically perpetuate the already existing inequalities. It is obligatory on the part of any governing structure or civil society to take affirmative, positive and pro-active steps to uplift the weaker, handicapped and marginalized sections of society so that they can take benefit on equal footing.

Rights of Minorities Under Indian Constitution

Knowing fully well that the Indian society had geological layers, the framers of Indian Constitution kept safeguards for the handicapped sections of the society especially the Scheduled Castes and Scheduled Tribes, Backward Classes and Religious and Linguistic Minorities. It is heartening to know that the Indian Constitution permits positive discrimination in favour of weak, disadvantaged and backward sections of the society. Article 14 ensures equality before the law and equal protection by the law whereas the Articles 15 and 16 Prohibits discrimination on the grounds of religion, race, caste, sex and place of birth. Article 15 permits the State to make "any special provisions" for women, children, any socially and educationally backward class of citizens and Scheduled Castes and Scheduled Tribes. The Article 15 has been recently amended by the Constitution (Ninety-third Amendment Act, 2005) to empower the State to make special provisions, by law, for admission of socially and educationally backward classes of citizens or Scheduled Castes/Scheduled Tribes to educational institutions, whether aided or unaided by the State, other than minority educational institutions. Article 16 also has an enabling clause that allows the State to make provisions for the reservations in appointments of posts in favour of any backward class of citizens, which in the opinion of State, is not adequately represented in the services under the State. Under Article 16(4) economic criteria by itself is not enough, the economic backwardness of the backward class has to be on account of educational and social backwardness. Thus, reservation or any positive discrimination under Indian conditions as per the spirit of Indian Constitution is permissible on the ground of caste or religion provided it is coupled with other grounds such as social and educational backwardness. Even in the Directive Principle of State Policy, Article 46 mandates the State "to promote with special care the educational and economic interests of the weaker sections of the people." It is also stated that the State "shall protect them from social injustice and all forms of exploitation." Apparently, this Article refers to

Scheduled Castes/Scheduled Tribes in particular but does not debar other weaker sections of the society from the benefits provided under this Article. Though Article 340 of the Constitution did not make it mandatory but empowered the President of India to appoint a Commission to investigate the conditions of socially and educationally backward classes.

In the same way, Article 21 states that no person shall be deprived of his life or personal liberty except through the procedure established by law. Article 25 ensures freedom of conscience and the right to freely profess, practice and propagate religion. Article 26 ensures right to manage religious institutions, religious affairs subject to public order, morality and health. Article 27 ensures freedom as to payment of taxes for promotion of any particular religion and Article 28 provides freedom as to attendance at religious instruction or religious worship in certain educational institutions. Article 29 protects the rights of minorities to conserve their language, script or culture. Article 29 provides that:

(1) Any section of the citizens residing in the territory of India or any part thereof having a distinct language, script or culture of its own shall have the right to conserve the same, and

(2) No citizen shall be denied admission into any educational institution maintained by the State or receiving aid out of State funds on grounds of religion, race, caste, language or any of them.

Article 30 provides for the protection of the interests of the minorities by giving them a right to establish and administer educational institutions of their choice. The State is directed not to discriminate against minorities in granting aid. Clause (1-A0) of the Article 30 was inserted in the Constitution as Constitution (Forty-fourth Amendment) Act, 1978 providing that "in making any law providing for the compulsory acquisition of any property of an educational institution established and administered by a minority, referred to in Clause (1), the State shall ensure that the amount fixed by or determined under such law for the acquisition of such property in such as would not restrict or abrogate the right guaranteed under that clause." It is worth noting that minority educational institutions under Clause of (1) of Article 30, have been protected from the purview of Article 15(4) of the Constitution which empowers the State to make provisions by law for the advancement of any socially and educationally backward classes of citizens or SCs/STs in regard to their admissions to educational institutions including private educational institutions whether aided or not. It is interesting to note that the rights of minorities to establish and administer educational institutions of their choice were to be protected by Clause (6) of Article 19 or Article 19(1)(g) but with a view to instill confidence among minorities and to protect them from any legislative or executive encroachment, the Article 30 was introduced. Besides, Articles 347 and 350 also provide protection to linguistic minorities inhabiting a State helping them to preserve and propagate their language. Article 347 states that on a demand being made in that behalf, the President may, if he is satisfied that a substantial proportion of the population of a State desire the use of any language spoken by them to be recognized by the State , direct that such language shall also be officially recognized throughout that State or any part thereof. Article 350 provides that every person shall be entitled to submit a representation for the redress of any grievance to any officer of authority of the Union or a State in any of the languages used in the Union or in the State as the case may be. Similarly, Article 350-A of the Constitution provides that "it shall be the endeavour of every State and every local authority within the State to provide adequate facilities for instruction in the mother-tongue at the primary stage of education to children belonging to linguistic minority groups; and the President may issue such direction to any State as he considers necessary or proper for securing the provision of such facility." Likewise, Article 350-B provides for appointment of Special Officer for linguistic minorities by the President. It shall be the duty of the Special Officer to investigate all matters relating to the safeguards provided for linguistic minorities under the Constitution and report to the President upon those matters at such intervals as the President may direct. All such reports are required to be laid before each house of Parliament, and also sent to Governments of States concerned. Thus, we find that there are enough safeguards for the protection of minorities and Muslims can take the advantage of the relevant provisions depending upon the situation.

The Government of India and several other State Governments have opened many institutions for the betterment of the minorities but they mostly proved merely the paper tigers as most of them lacked constitutional powers. For instance, with a view to evaluating the progress of minorities and monitoring the safeguards provided in the Constitution as well as looking into specific complaints and causing studies pertaining to discrimination and conducting studies, suggesting appropriate measures and making periodical reports, the Central Government had instituted a non-statutory Minorities Commission in 1978. In 1992, the National Commission for Minorities was enacted to provide for constitution of a statutory Commission. The National Commission for Minorities was established under the Act in 1993. Muslims of India were not happy with the said Commission for it had no teeth. A Constitution Amendment Bill, viz, the Constitution (One Hundred and Third Amendment) Bill, 2004 has been introduced so as to add a new Article 340-A to constitute a National Commission for Minorities with a constitutional status. A Bill to repeal the National Commission for Minorities Act, 1992 has been simultaneously introduced. Justice Misra Commission feels that the National Commission for Minorities Act, 1992 needs to be suitably amended with a view to include in it the provisions similar to Article 338(9) and 383A(9) so that it may be mandatory on the part of the Union and every State Government to consult the National Commission for Minorities on all major policy matters affecting the minorities. Besides, there is a need for the provision for a reasonable time frame for the recommendations to be laid, along with memorandum of action taken before the Parliament/State Legislature and also there is a case for laying down definite time frame for laying the annual reports for the Commission on the tables of both Houses of Parliament along with action taken reports. Likewise, the National Commission for Minority Educational Institutions Act, 2004 was enacted pertaining to complaints regarding deprivation or violation of rights of minorities to establish and administer educational institutions of their choice, disputes pertaining to affiliations and its findings to the appropriate Government for implementation. However, in the opinion of the Commission, there is a need to make clear-cut, concrete and positive recommendations for improving and streamlining the provisions of the Act. The Muslim intelligentsia also strongly feel that the provisions of Prevention of Atrocities (SC/ST) Act, 1989 need to be extended so as to cover OBCs, Minorities and other marginalized socially and economically backward sections of the society to protect them from the discrimination and atrocities and persecution by the non-backward and privileged sections of the society.

Various Welfare Measures for the Betterment of Minorities

The ancient Indian society based on value system and the dynamic Indian Constitution upholding the long traditions of secularism, socialism and humanism provided special provisions to protect the cultural and educational rights of minorities. The young State respecting diversities among different sections, religions, faiths, belief systems, ethnic groups, cultural conglomerations and believing in the dictum of "Vasudeva Kutumbakam launched development programmes for removing past distortions of extreme nature from the highly iniquitous social stratified structure of complex Indian society through conscious policy of intervention. Since the Constitution provides a strong socio-legal framework for removal of old disparities, efforts were made through planned development to achieve de facto equality via equity and social justice measures and policies. The planners were committed to principles of social justice and respect for diversity and absolute and unconditional equality for all faiths. They also believed in the protection of the fundamental rights of all communities and preserving their composite culture, promoting the spirit of harmony and brotherhood respecting the mosaic of different streams of a plural society. Initially the strategy of government of India was to bring the economy at par with Pre-partition days since it had been derailed due to the Partition of the country and the ensuing communal riots and mass migration of the people across borders. The second purpose was to give a proper direction to its socio-economic and politico-cultural values and utilize its dormant resources for the benefit of its people which were previously exploited by the British in distorted manner for the betterment of their people and the country. Thus, Five Year Plans were launched to increase GDP, Per Capita Income, achieve regional balance, lessen inequalities and achieve balanced growth and development of the country. The focus was mainly on overall development as well as sectoral and regional growth rather than on individual, class or group amelioration. In the earlier, phase a separate focus on minorities was not considered necessary for the planners wanted the inclusive development of all societies through poverty alleviation, rural and urban employment, aiming at income generation in the hope that the mechanism of planning would unleash a process of growth for all-round development including the development of minorities. Very soon it was felt that a purposeful development mechanism was necessary for the growth and development of weaker sections of society especially the Scheduled Castes and Scheduled Tribes for they had remained in the state of exploitation for centuries. Several welfare measures were taken specifically for the benefit of Scheduled Castes, Scheduled Tribes, Backward Castes and Below the Poverty Line people. The intention perhaps was that those communities which were marginalized, depressed and isolated would also take the advantage of some of the schemes which were specifically marked for Below Poverty Line masses but the Muslims as a big minority could not take the benefit of those measures despite being forming the significant portion of the marginalized and depressed communities. Later on it was felt that the minorities of the country too needed a tailor-made programmes for their betterment since they were the vital part of Indian society but were not made the integral part of the planning process. Keeping in mind the problems of the minorities various policies were followed which benefitted the minorities to a large extent but Muslims failed to take the advantage of such schemes too due to their faulty implementations. The facts emerged on the scene that Muslims had fallen far behind the national average practically among all parameters especially, education and employment in Government and private sector and the large segment of the society was frustrated due to poverty, discrimination and deprivation. Efforts were then made in the Tenth Five Year

Plan (2002-07) through separate Minority Development Programmes by sparing peanut amount for the benefit of Muslims. It is the misfortune of Indian Muslims that no government could muster courage to announce any meaningful programmes purely for Muslims on the pattern of ventures launched for SCs/STs and Backward Castes involving huge resources due to fear of backlash from the rightist parties. Most of the programmes were launched sparing meager resources directly for all the minorities of the country but the impression was given to the Muslims that they were primarily for them. Since there was all round bias against Muslims in the country in one form or other especially at implementation stage, the minority development programmes neither came in the notice of large sections of Muslims, nor were they implemented in letter and spirit. Dr. Gopal Singh Committee held that Muslims and the Neo-Buddhists were two educationally most backward minorities at national level and needed special measures to bring them within national mainstream. Ironically, Neo Buddhist since then has been placed at par with the SC population for getting all the benefits but Muslims were left where they were. The National Policy on Education 1986 highlighted the fact that some minority groups especially the Muslims were educationally backward or deprived. The Sachar Committee noted with grief the pathetic literacy rate, lower socio-economic status, extreme poverty, higher unemployment, meager infrastructure and very poor representation in civil services and deprivation in the field of industry, trade and commerce. It is highly frustrating that despite this, save cosmetic measures here and there no definite steps have been taken by the governing structure and the civil society for the betterment of Muslims, inadvertently giving the impression as if they are perhaps others.

The Government is claiming that it is endeavouring to focus on Minority-dominated areas, ensuring adequate representation of minority communities in employment under Central and State as well as Public Sector Undertakings; ensuring flow of benefits to the minority communities under maintenance and development of religious Wakf properties and redresser of grievances of minorities. It is emphasized that greater resources for teaching Urdu have been released, modernization of Madarsa education is on the top list of the government, scholarship to meritorious students are being regularly given, educational infrastructure is being improved through Maulana Azad Foundation. Besides, the coaching classes in minority institutions and polytechnics in minority dominated areas have been started to provide them training. Moreover, recruitment to State and Central Services, equitable share in rural housing, improvement in conditions of slums, prevention and control of communal riots, prosecution of communal offences, special courts to expedite communal offences and rehabilitation of victims of communal riots were on the priority list of the government. In addition to it, they claim that the general programmes meant for all populations such as Sarvshiksha Abhiyan, Swarnajayanti Sahari Rozgar Yojna, Indira Awas Yojna, Sampoorna Grameen Rozgar Yojna, National Rural Health Commission, Jawahar Lal Nehru Urban Renewal Mission, National Slum Development Programme, Bharat Nirman Programme, National Rural Employment Guarantee Programme, National Commission on Farmers, National Horticulture Mission, Joint Forest Management, etc. are also helping the betterment of the minorities. They forget that the common programmes could not benefit Muslims since they were mostly launched in majority dominated areas where many Muslims hesitated to go. Besides, Muslims being educationally and economically backward could not take the advantage of such programmes which needed some minimum abilities or qualifications at preparatory stage. Over and above this, Muslims were not aware of most of such programmes as seldom any NGO's tried to approach Muslims and convince them about their utilities.

The ground situation, however, is that as a result of overall development of the country through planning and through specific development projects for SCs/STs and Backward Castes the ratio of SCs and STs below poverty line has been decreased but the incidence of poverty among Muslims in urban areas is the highest and the greater number of backward Muslims such as Ajlafs and Arzals comprise such occupation groups such as carpenters, artisans, painters, grazers, tanners, milkmen and the lowest among them consist of Halakhor, Lalbegi, Abdal and Bediya. In matters of poverty, education and employment, Muslim community is on the lowest pedestal. At most, it may be compared to SCs/STs or BPL families. Majority of the Muslim-concentrated districts fall within the most backward regions in north of Vindhayas. They are far behind in terms of economic progress, access to basic infrastructure, share of decision making and the protection of their cultural values. There is more or less complete absence of information pertaining to the benefits received by minorities through various minority-oriented programmes. No affirmative steps have been taken to reach to the poorest among the poor. Essentially, there is a need of proper data bank to collect statistics regarding education, employment, training, productive credit, political participation and social and economic development of minorities. The National Minority Development and Finance Corporation is starving due to the lack of funds. Only 1.6% eligible minority candidates have received financial support. Several state governments have not opened Minority Welfare Departments as well as State Minorities Commissions and independent Minorities Development and Finance Corporations. There is meager representation of Muslims on State level Commissions, Committees, Boards and Corporations. Besides, the State Wakf Boards are short of funds, minority institutions face severe difficulties in getting registration and minority-run institutions are suffering due to lack of grants from government agencies. Government is coming out with liberal assistance for Madarsa education but it is being despised by majority of Muslims for they fear foul play behind the scheme. There is paucity of hostel and residential schools for minorities in major Muslim concentrated districts. There is decline of several old trade and professions which have severely affected Muslims. There is a need of counseling-cum- guidance centre for entrepreneurs and artisans as well as a cell to monitor the implementation of various schemes including the Prime Minister's 15-Point Programme. Finally, there is an urgency to have a legal mechanism to ensure that the minority communities get fair deal in recruitment and employment.

(A) Critique of Welfare Measures for the Development of Minorities

It is often emphasized by the ruling governments that

efforts were made by the Central and the State Governments through planning and development policies to reach to the basic problems of minorities such as education, health, infrastructure, employment, social transformation and cultural enrichment through poverty alleviation, income generation, rural and urban development and socio-cultural and socio-economic empowerment. The objective of all these strategies was the welfare and the well being of all the citizens of the country irrespective of religion, caste and class. Since these schemes were largely for the betterment of the poor and the depressed sections of the society, they were also destined to benefit educationally, socially and economically backward segments from among the minorities. The fact is that these schemes have benefitted the least to the Muslims. In order to obtain a realistic picture and find out the impact of such policies of the governments and identify gaps between physical and financial targets and achievements, some of the important schemes have been analyzed in the following section.

(b) General Schemes for the Growth of All Segments of Society

It is claimed that the government took several steps to strengthen the educational base of the minorities after Independence among which the National Literacy Mission was set up in 1988 to attain a high and sustainable literacy level among people through integrated approach. It is also held that the achievement of NLM was marvelous as the literacy rate among minorities rose to 70.30 per cent in 2001 and the gender gap in literacy too came down to12.56 per cent during the same time. As a matter of fact the Christians, Sikhs, Jains and Buddhists got benefit since the educational attainment levels were highest among Jains, followed by Christians, Sikhs, Hindus and Buddhists. Unfortunately Muslims were at the lowest level. The literacy rate among 7 + population of Muslim was lowest among Muslim males and females as well as rural and urban males and females compared to all segments of the majority community including all other minorities save the SCs/STs. Likewise, educational attainment among Muslims both males and females was lower than all communities including the SCs/STs and other minorities at Middle, Secondary, Senior Secondary, Diploma and graduate levels. Similarly, Muslim children could not take the benefit of

Kendriya Vidyalayas(KVs) and Navodaya Vidyalayas(NVs) for their proportion at Secondary and Senior Secondary was merely to the extent of 10.96% and 4.53% respectively. Besides, these institutions had reserved seats for the SCs and STs in proportion to their population in concerned districts to a maximum of 50%. Besides, SC and ST students were provided bridge courses and other facilities of schooling for those who had missed opportunities. Muslim students being in reasonable number at Primary level could take the advantage of Mid-day Meal Scheme (National Programme of Nutritional Support to Primary Education) launched in 1995 like all other students including SCs/STs covering nearly 12 crore children in over 8 lakh schools. However, the Vocational Education Schemes to teach various courses including various crafts, health and Paramedical, Horticulture, Agriculture, Fisheries, Insurance, computer science, rural marketing and Home Science benefitted the Muslim students least because very few Muslim students possessed National vocational education qualifications. In the same way, the post-Matric Scholarship to provide financial support to Scheduled Castes, Scheduled Tribes and other Backward Classes to pursue studies beyond Matriculation and pre-Matric Scholarship meant for Scheduled Caste/Scheduled Tribe mainly benefitted the SC/ST students and the students from the Backward Castes. Muslim students were conspicuous by their absence. Moreover, the National Overseas Scholarship Scheme could not help Muslim students as it was available for Scheduled Castes/Scheduled Tribes/De-notified Nomadic students for up gradation of Merit Scheme. Hostel assistance was also provided to minority students but Muslims could not take its advantage because their number at Middle, Higher Secondary and College level was insignificant. The Higher and Technical Education Scheme of University Grant Commission too was irrelevant for Muslim students for the UGC had earmarked quota of 15 per cent for SCs and 7.5 per cent for STs in appointments in teaching and non-teaching posts, admissions, hostel accommodation in Universities/ colleges. The UGC also provides financial assistance for remedial coaching to SC and ST students for undergraduate and postgraduate students and for preparing for the NET (National Eligibility Test). The UGC has provided some assistance to disadvantaged Minority groups to prepare for various competitive examinations but this scheme too is benefitting only a fragment of the Muslim society. Indira Gandhi National Open University is providing various courses to all sections of the society including the minorities and Muslim students are benefitting from these courses to some extent. However, the Community Polytechnics meant for training unemployed rural youth, minorities, SCs/STs, women, school droppers and other disadvantaged sections have benefitted least to Muslim students due to their meager number and their compulsion to work to supplement the income of the family. Since the above mentioned Schemes were mostly focused on the educational development of SC and ST students, they have shown results. During 1980-81 to 2003-04 the enrolment of SC students has increased from 11 million to 23 million in primary classes; from 2.2 million to 8 million at the Middle level and from 1.1 million to 4.8 million at the secondary stage and girls formed 44.8%, 41.4% and 38.2% at these levels respectively. The ST children too have gained much as during 1980-81 to 2003-04 the enrolment of Scheduled Tribe children rose from 4.6 million to 12.5 million in primary classes; from 0.74 million to 3.7 million at middle level and from 0.33 million to 1.95 million at the secondary stage and the girls formed 45.9%, 41.7% and 37.4% at these different levels respectively. The impact of this revolution was that the Scheduled Castes and the Scheduled Tribes emerged from the dogmatic slumber and became the active part in the mainstream and the Muslims due to lack of patronage slipped in the vacuum created by them.

The Government has also started two employment generation credit-linked subsidy schemes namely the Rural Employment Generation Programme (REGP) and Prime Minister's Rozgar Yojna (PMRY). It is claimed that since its inception in 1995 till March 2005, the Employment Generation Programme has financed 2,09,705 projects and created 28.06 lakh additional job opportunities. Nearly 12.4% SCs, 5.7% STs and 23.8% Other Backward Classes have been benefitted out of which 25.8% were women beneficiaries. Incidentally, the minorities too have been benefitted to the extent of 12.8% but the share of Muslims in this venture too remained negligible.

Likewise, it is said that under Prime Minister's Rozgar Yojana loans were disbursed to 22.80 lakhs self-employment ventures, creating jobs for 34.20 lakhs persons. During 1993-99 the proportion of beneficiaries from SCs/STs was 21% and that of OBCs was 26%. As can be seen from the above statistics that the figures have been given about the SCs/STs and the Backward Castes from which it cannot be concluded that many of the beneficiaries were Muslims. It has been generally seen that among minorities and Backward Castes the chances of other than Muslims are brighter compared to Muslims. In the same way, the Sampoorna Grameen Rozgar Yojana (SGRY) launched in 2001 too was primarily meant for providing additional wage employment in rural areas to women, SCs, STs and parents of children withdrawn from hazardous occupations. In this scheme 22.5% of the annual allocation was meant for individual/group beneficiaries schemes for SC/ST and a minimum of 50% of the Village Panchayat allocation was earmarked for the creation of need based village infrastructure for SC/ST habitations and wards. The Scheme has annual allocation of Rs. 6000 crores and 50 lakh tonnes of food grains. In this venture the participation of Muslims is practically nil. It is primarily meant for SCs/STs and other rural poor and rural women labourers. During 2004-05 nearly 50 lakh tones of food grains was released, expenditure to the extent of Rs. 6018.09 crores was incurred and 8223.09 lakh man days of work created and 1639619 works completed. The Swarnjayanti Gram SwaerozgarYojana (SGSY) too could not benefit Muslims for it was stipulated that at least 50% beneficiaries will be Scheduled Castes/Scheduled Tribes, 40% women and 3% disabled. Likewise, the National Food for Work Programme, National Rural Employment Guarantee Act (NREGA), Enhancing Employment Potential in Agriculture Sector and Enhancing Employment Potential in Industrial Sector as well as National Commission for Enterprises in Unorganized Sector, Council for Advancement of People's Action and Rural Technology and Small and Agro-Rural Industries benefitted the SCs/STs and the Backward Castes in the villages and Muslims could not take any benefit out of them.

(c) Specific Schemes for Minorties

If we now analyze the Schemes specifically meant for Minorities we would find that the Government had provided peanuts for minorities in budgets for their uplift compared to the huge amount provided for the growth and development of Scheduled Castes and Scheduled Tribes as well as the Backward Castes .Since the Parliament and State Assemblies are mostly composed by a large segment from the SCs/STs and Backward Castes, they can exert political pressure for the development of their respective constituencies. However, as Muslims have practically no constituencies of their own and reach Parliament or Assemblies on the support of others, they cannot put any pressure from their side for the betterment of Muslims. Moreover, since Muslims are spread throughout the country and have no reserved quota, as a group or a community they have no say in the Parliament or the Assemblies but depend upon the mercy of the Governments at the Centre and the States. From the budgeted amounts allocated for the amelioration of Muslims it is abundantly clear that the Central Government as well as State Governments have not put Muslims on the same pedestal as SCs/STs and OBCs Out of the Budgetary Support for operating the New 15 Point Programme an allocation of Rs.63 crores was earmarked for the National Minorities Development and Finance Corporation over last year's Rs. 16.47 crores. The budget also provided 108 crores for multi-sector development programmes for minority dominated areas. Three different scholarships have been introduced for minority students in which Rs. 72 crores have been allocated for Pre-Matric scholarship, Rs. 90 crores for post-matric scholarship and Rs. 48.60 crores for graduates and post-graduate level. It is interesting to know that since its inception during the last twenty five years, the National Minority Development and Finance Corporation has provided financial assistance of Rs. 917.75 crores to 3,41,077 families through State Channelizing Agencies and NGOs. The total number of beneficiaries up to 2006-07 was 2,17,071 persons with a total disbursement of Rs. 9818.00 lakhs. The NMDFC up to 31st March, 2005 covered merely 1.60% of those eligible to receive economic development support under the programme. Incidentally, out of the meagre funds, 77% of funds under term loan and Micro-Finance were provided to Muslims followed by 15% to Christians and 7.5% for Sikhs. Uttar Pradesh availed 19.31%, West Bengal, 15.90% and Kerala 14.29%. Similarly, among the State-wise Disbursement of loans and beneficiaries coverage (Term loan only) cumulative as on 31st March 2005, the coverage of Andhra Pradesh was 9.71%, Gujarat 7.50%, Karnataka 7.98%,Kerala 13.36% Mizoram 5.55% Uttar Pradesh 17.46% and West Bengal 16.12%. The remaining 11 states received less than1% and 9 of them received below 3%.The bank credit to minorities too has been meagre. The status of Credit Disbursement to minorities in 41 minority concentrated districts by Scheduled Commercial banks reveals an increase of accounts in the five year period to the tune of 19237, showing a growth of merely 1.31%. The proportion of Muslims in 41 districts was 33.35% but the small average amount per loan availed was due to their lower credit absorption capacity which could be because of the lack of necessary skill and knowledge of trade as well the difficulty in getting loans. The National Bank for Agriculture and Rural Development (NABARD) financed to the tune of Rs.3085.91 crores by 31st March 2005 enabling 242.5 lakh poor household to gain access to micro finance from formal banking. Similarly, Small Industrial Development Bank of India (SIDBI) too sanctioned loans up to 31st March 2005 to the extent of Rs. 527 crores under the micro credit programme in favour of 22 lakh beneficiaries but Muslims participation among all these ventures remained negligible.

More or less the same was the fate of other Institutions specifically promoted for the betterment of Minorities. For instance, Maulana Azad Education Foundation (MAEF) which was set up in 1989 for the promotion of education among educationally backward minorities had a corpus fund of merely Rs. 200 crores and since its inception it had sanctioned grant-in –aid of Rs. 93.42 crores to 718 NGOs all over the country. During 2005-06 the Foundation had released scholarship amounting to Rs. 10.82 crores covering 10832 beneficiaries.

The Foundation is also running vocational training centre at Ajmeri Gate Delhi to impart training to about 250 women in cutting, tailoring, designing, arts and crafts. Likewise, The Central Wakf Council, a statutory body executes various charity and educational programmes among weaker sections of Muslims. It received merely grant-in-aid amounting to Rs.28.20 crores up to the year 2005-06 and extended loans to the extent of Rs. 28.47 crores to 14 States up to March 2005. Besides, the Council also awarded 10802 scholarships up to March 2006 to students of technical degree courses. The National Council for Promotion of Urdu Language a registered body helps to establish a link between the Urdu-speaking population with technical and vocational education. The Council has received a grant of Rs. 82.21 crores from the Government since 1996. It has established several Computer Application and Multilingual DTP centres and these centres have produced 13,161 girl students as medium level professionals during the last five years. The National Commission of Minority Educational Institution was set up in 2004 to advise the Centre and State Governments on any matter regarding establishment and administration of educational institutions. It has been working as an advisory body and has received several complaints from Muslim institutions facing problems pertaining to establishment and running the minority institutions. The National Monitoring Committee for Minorities was reconstituted in August 2004 and it has submitted its report in 2005 which is under the consideration of the Government. The Scheme of Area Intensive programme for Educationally Backward Minorities and the Scheme of Financial Assistance for Modernization of Madarsa Education were merged in the Tenth Plan in a new Scheme called the Area Intensive Madarsa Modernization Programme (AIMM). The Tenth Plan allocation for AIMM schemes was to the tune of Rs. 83.92 crores and the expenditure during 2002-03 and 2003-04 and 20004-05 was Rs. 28.45 crores, Rs. 29.00 crores and Rs. 22 crores respectively. In 2004-05 the expenditure of Rs. 22 crores was incurred for the construction of 11 hostels for girls, 11 senior secondary buildings and payment of salaries to teachers for teaching modern subjects in 575 madarsas.The Sarva Shiksha Abhiyan (SSA) was designed for the spread of elementary education of satisfactory quality with emphasis on education for life for children in age group 6-14 years. The SSA has identified 93 districts in 16 States for special attention to educate minority children. During 2005-06 the SSA sanctioned 2643 primary schools, 1978 upper primary schools and 2900 EGS centres. Looking to the fact that India has the second largest educational system in the world next to China, these half-hearted measures to satisfy Muslims are mere gimmicks. The country has total enrolment of 222.03 million out of which 45% are girls. Besides, girls form 47% of the 128.27 million children enrolled in primary classes; 44.4% of the 48.73 million at middle range; 41.12 % of the 35 million at high/higher secondary stage and 39.68% of the 10 million students enrolled in institutions of higher learning. Not only this, during 1950-51 to 2003-04 the enrolment at primary level has gone up from 19.2 million to 128.3 million; at middle level from 3.1 million to 48.7 million and from 1.5 million to 35 million at high/higher secondary level. The enrolment of Scheduled Caste children in primary classes went up from 11 million in 1880-81 to 2003-04; from 2.2 million to 8 million at the middle stage and from1.1million to 4.8 million at secondary level during the same period. The Scheduled Tribe students too have gone up from 4.6 million to 12.5 million in primary classes; from 0.74 million to 3.7 million at middle stage and from 0.33 million to 1.95 million at the secondary stage between 1980-81 and 2003-04. In this race of accelerated growth Muslims stand nowhere. During 2006 the number of Muslim children age group 6-13 going to schools was 2,25,94,419 compared to 3,80,20,794 for SCs, 1,73,70,283 for ST, 6,66,69,095 for OBC and 4,93,74,053 for others. The number of Muslim children out of school was 12.03% in rural areas compared to 4.39% for others, 7.73% for OBCs, 8.55% for SCs and 10.11% for STs. likewise in urban areas 7.7% were out of schools compared to 6.25% SCs, 4.21% STs, 3.83% OBCs and 2.44% for others. This situation is after the fact that Muslim parents are taking active interest across the line for the educational development of their children after knowing the pitiable condition of their community fellows.

A study on 'Socio-economic Status of Minorities- Factors for their Backwardness was conducted by Centre for Research, Planning and Action, New Delhi in urban areas of five states i.e. Maharashtra, Punjab, Tamil Nadu, Uttar Pradesh and West Bengal spread over 15 cities selected on the basis of high concentration of religious minorities covering households with income up to Rs. 3000/- per month. The results indicate that 35.68% minority population had no formal education. Graduates were merely 5.82% and post-graduates constituted just 1.26%. Besides, the ratio of those with no formal education was as high as 71% among Muslim families. Another study conducted by AROH Foundation, New Delhi on the Educational Status of Minorities revealed that Muslim families do not enroll their children in regular schools. The 6.3% of Muslim children in the age group of 7-19 years who study in Maktabs and Madarsas suffer as they cannot compete with the school going children and find it difficult to enter in the mainstream education system after completing their Maktab and Madarsa education. It was observed that Muslims do not attach too much importance to modern education because they are convinced that their children would remain unemployed after getting education. They send their children to Madarsas to acquire religious education which they deem necessary for their children in this world and in the hereafter. Besides, they cannot afford the modern costly education as most of their time is passed without any gainful activities. They prefer engaging their children in hereditary professions or in mechanical or technical or hawkers' jobs to supplement their incomes and to meet their two ends.

In the end we may conclude that most of the Muslims of India are indeed a depressed, neglected and dejected lot. They are far behind the other segments of the society including the Scheduled Castes, Scheduled Tribes and Backward Castes in almost all the parameters which determine the growth and development of any caste, class, group or community. There is a lack of an institutional framework to support them in their genuine ventures. There is practically no data bank to collect facts and figures to determine their status as the marginalized and backward sections of society. There is hardly any legal support system to help them in ameliorating their educational, social and economic conditions. There is invariably no political class to assist them during their lean days and they seldom get any moral support from the civil society despite the fact that they are the most neglected part of Indian society. Several Muslim organizations such as Jamat-e-Islami Hind, Darul Uloom(Wakf) Deoband, All India Muslim Majls-E-Mushawarat, All India Jamiat-Ur-Rayeen, All India Jamaat –e-Saifia, All India Jamiatul Quresh, All India Momin Conference and Muslim Educational, Social and Cultural Organisation (MESCO) and many more from various parts of the country are there but mostly they involve themselves in the social and religious affairs of Muslims and fail to attract the attention of the governing structure and the meaningful sections of Indian society towards the miserable condition of Muslims.

Ironically, the Planning Commission and various government agencies have neither allocated sufficient funds for their development commensurate to their share in population nor the Central and State Government made any affirmative endeavours to provide them admissions in schools, colleges, universities and technical institutes as well as employment in government and semi-government organizations and representations in Parliament, State Assemblies and district and village level bodies in proportion to their share in the nations' demographic strength to wipe out the development deficit. Many of them are not aware of health, educational, financial and other promotional schemes for their growth and development. Several are living in depleted houses for nobody helped them in getting the benefits of various rehabilitation and slum development programmes and housing schemes meant for the up lift of the poor. Their Urdu schools are suffering from insufficiency of infrastructure, lack of motivation, absence of appropriate text books, non fulfilling of vacancies and paucity of funds. Nearly 36% Muslims are below Poverty Line compared to national average of 26%, literacy rate and work participation is lower amongst them as against other minorities and the national average and they are mostly small and marginal farmers, landless agricultural labourers, petty traders, hawkers and craftsmen. They are facing downward mobility due to the fact that their traditional professions and vocations are not compatible with modern development. They have highest dependency ratio due to highest population of the young in the age group 0-14 years and the lowest proportion of the working population. They suffer from financial crunch because the formal financial sector has no special schemes or credit targets for Muslims. Despite the fact that Muslims constitute largest minority community comprising 13.43% of the total population and 72.92% of minorities population of the country yet they are one of the most marginalized and deprived communities in India in terms of education, income, employment, health, infrastructure and socio-economic and politico-cultural indices. The credit goes to Justice Ranganath Misra Commission for suggesting affirmative steps including reservation for Muslims in government jobs and educational institutions as provided to Scheduled Castes and Scheduled Tribes and Backward Classes, being educationally, socially and economically backward and weakest, marginalised and downtrodden compared to all segments of the society. The time will only show what part the Government would play to salvage the conditions of Muslims in our country.

2

The Empowerment of Scheduled Castes, Scheduled Tribes and Other Backward Classes Through Reservations

It is the law of nature, irony of fate and the fact of history that all people are not born equal in every respect. Few are born rich with silver spoons in their mouths, some with wisdom and genius at their command, many with tainted destiny, several with blank fate sheet, innumerable with handicaps and multitude with debit balances. Some assign their adverse beginning to their past Karmas, believers impute it to the ingenious plan of their Lord and the agnostics apportion it to the chance phenomena. However, one thing can be said without any shred of doubt that every religion and every civilized society has always been kind and considerate to those born as marginalized, backward and less privileged sections of the society. The framers of Indian Constitution too were aware of the fact that Indian society had distinguishing marks in the sense that it had geological layers and many of its citizens were handicapped due to accidents of history, traditional backgrounds and socio-cultural norms. Since they were born with inequalities and disabilities of various kinds they could not enjoy the equality of status or of opportunity as enshrined in Indian Constitution. The beauty of Indian Constitution is that equality pervades throughout the Constitution since the founders of the Constitution wanted to establish an egalitarian society in India wherein social, economic and political justice could be enjoyed by all without any kind of discrimination and each and every citizen of the country could enjoy the equality of status and opportunity despite possessing religious, social, cultural and historical differences. Various Articles of Indian Constitution allow protective, positive and affirmative discrimination in favour of marginalized sections of the society with a view to remove the persistent or present and continuing effects of past discriminations or handicaps and disabilities in matters of access to equal opportunities. They also grant equality of status and provide opportunity for fuller participation in governing structure by removing substantial chronic under-participation or under-representation and help them to serve or achieve the important constitutional or governmental objectives

The History of Reservation

The history of reservation in India is very old. Reservation of seats for marginalized and depressed sections of the society were in vogue since long. After the 1857 War of Independence, the British had realized that Indian society was a conglomeration of various heterogeneous groups which materially differed in matters of educational, social and economic empowerment. They provided special benefits to the religious minorities and lower castes. By the late nineteenth century they prepared a list of depressed classes and started schools and other programmes including providing scholarships in different courses and jobs in government departments for the less privileged and neglected segments of the society. In Mumbai the government reserved seats for all sections of the society considering them backward and excluded Brahmins, Marwaris, Banias, Parsis and Christians treating them as forward and privileged. In 1927 the Government reserved 5 out of every 12 jobs for non-Brahman Hindus,. 2 each for Brahmins, Christians and Muslims and 1 for others in Madras Presidency. Some of the princely states like Baroda, Travancore and Kolhapur and Mysore too provided educational facilities to untouchables and the backwards. Mahatma Jyotirao Phuley was the first reformer in India who started a school for the untouchables in Pune in 1948. Similarly, Sahuji Maharaj

Bhonsale encouraged the non-Brahminical classes to pursue education as a means for socio-economic development. He provided free education along with scholarships and lodging, boarding and other facilities. In Kolhapur 50% vacant posts were reserved by Sahuji Maharaj for non-Brahmans. The Princely State of Mysore had instituted a mechanism in which all communities other than Brahmins were denominated "Backward Classes and from 1918 seats were reserved for them in colleges and State services. At the official level, the Madras Government framed the Grants-in-Aid Code in 1885 to regulate financial aid to the educational institutions providing facilities to depressed and the marginalized sections of society. In 1944 the Ministry of Education prepared a scheme of post-matric scholarship for Scheduled Caste students and extended the same to the students of Scheduled Tribe in 1948. After Independence the Ministry of Education directed the State Governments in 1954 to reserve 20% seats for Scheduled Caste and Scheduled Tribe students in admissions in educational institutions with a provision of providing 5% relaxation in minimum qualifying marks. Subsequently the 20% limit was modified in April 1964 so as to provide the benefit to the extent of 15% to Scheduled Castes and 5% to Scheduled Tribes with interchangeable provision in the event of non-fulfillment of seats according to quota. Similar measures were taken by Ministry of Health and Family Welfare to provide reservation in universities having medical and dental facilities and colleges for admissions to all post-graduate courses. The University Grants Commission too did not lag behind. It made provisions for reservations in admissions at under-graduate and post-graduate level in favour of SC and ST students along with necessary relaxations and concessions. The percentage of reservation was revised in 1982 to provide 15% to Scheduled Castes and 7.5% for Scheduled Tribes.

(a) Reservation for Scheduled Castes and Scheduled Tribes

Initially, the British Government had reserved seats only in legislative bodies but due to continuous efforts of various segments of Depressed Classes and the special efforts of Dr. B.R Ambedkar reservations in Government jobs and services to the extent of 8.33% against direct recruitment through open competition were made for Scheduled Castes in 1943. After the country became free instructions were issued by the Government of India to reserve 12.5% posts for Scheduled Castes against direct recruitment made through open competition and 16.66% made for those other than open competition. After the promulgation of Constitution, 5% reservation for STs was made in services apart from the reservation for Scheduled Castes which had already been sanctioned. According to population ratio of SCs and STs based on 1961 Census, the Government of India on 25th March, 1970 increased the reserved seats from 12.5% and 5% to 15% and 7.5% in favour of SCs and STs respectively in direct recruitment on all -India basis through the UPSC or by means of open tests held by other authority. Scheduled Caste reservation was also provided to Sikhs and Buddhists and STs of all minorities as ST identity was caste or religion neutral. Besides, 16.66% and 7.5% reservation for SCs and STs was provided on 25th March, 1970 in case of direct recruitment on all-India basis by open competition otherwise than mentioned above. Reservation in promotion by selection from group C to group B, within group.B and from group B to lowest rung of group A was provided in 1974 with the proviso that the quantum of reservation did not exceed the limit of 50%. The limit of recruitment not exceeding 50% was raised to 66.66% in 1976 and then to 75% in 1989 to facilitate reservation in promotions. Following amendment of Constitution to incorporate Article 16(4A) in 1992, the Government of India issued instructions on 13.8.1997 that the reservations in promotions for SCs and STs, beyond15.11.1997 shall continue till such time as the representation of each of these categories in each cadre reaches to prescribed percentages. Needless to say that in order to fulfill the reservation quota for SCs and STs certain concessions and facilities have been provided in the form of relaxation of the maximum age limit for direct recruitment/ selection, exemption from payment of fees prescribed for recruitment/selection as well as relaxation of standards including relaxation of experience etc. Many of these concessions and relaxations have been provided for direct recruitment and have also now been extended to promotions to remove the deficit in the prescribed quota for reservations. The Scheduled Castes and the Scheduled Tribes give prime importance to education since in the opinion of Dr. B.R. Ambedkar education was the most important criteria to measure forwardness and backwardness. He advised them to give first and foremost importance to education considering it as "the milk of the lioness". Presently, apart from reservations in jobs and services, reservations to Scheduled Castes and Scheduled Tribes are also available in admissions to the various under-graduate and post-graduate courses in general streams, technical, medical and other professional courses in the colleges, institutes and universities. Besides admissions, the facilities for freeship, scholarship, coaching and hostel facilities are also available to these castes to strengthen their educational base. Moily Committee had recommended reservations for Other Backward Classes in educational Institutions and it is claimed that these recommendations have been accepted by the Government. However, reservation is not applicable to certain categories of posts in the Departments of Space and Atomic Energy, Scientific and Technical Personnel, Defence and Higher Judiciary etc.

(b) Reservation to Backward Classes

As far as reservations for Backward Classes are concerned, it is found that many states had made provisions for giving reservations to Backward Class people in services as well as admissions in educational institutions much earlier than Central Government came on the scene. For instance, in 1970 Andhra Pradesh provided 25% reservation in educational institutions and 25% in government services, Bihar in 1978 provided 24% in admissions and 20% in services, Gujarat sanctioned in 1976 to the tune of 10% in admissions and 10% in services and Jammu & Kashmir government took a decision in 1977 to give 42% reservation in educational Institutions and 42% in government services. Similarly, other States did not remain behind. Karnataka took initiative in1975 and provided 48% reservation in educational institutions and 50% in services. Kerala reserved 25% in admissions and 25% in services as far as 1953 and Punjab provided merely 5% in educational institutions and 5% in services in 1965. Maharashtra reserved 34% for educational institutions and 34% for services in the year 1964, Uttar Pradesh provided 15% in educational spheres and 15% in services since 1978 and Tamil Nadu was the pioneer in the sense that it had provided reservation to the Backward Classes in 1927 to the tune of 31% in educational institutions and 31% in services. As against this, Haryana provided 2% in admissions and 10% in services, Himachal Pradesh sanctioned merely 5% in services and Madhya Pradesh reserved 25% for educational institutions and 25% for services. The Government of India took initiative for providing reservation to Backward Classes by constituting Kaka Kalelkar Commission in 1953. The Commission submitted its report in 1955 listing 2399 Castes as educationally and socially backward and recommended several measures for their uplift including reservations in educational institutions and reservation of posts in government services. The Government of India did not accept the recommendations of Kaka Kalelkar Commissions since the cast-based reservations were considered a retrograde step by the government of India. The Second Backward Classes Commission popularly known as Mandal Commission was constituted by the Government of India in 1979 under Article 340 of the Constitution to analyze and investigate the conditions of educationally and socially backward classes and to determine the criteria to identify and define these classes and to examine the desirability or otherwise of making provisions for the reservation in favour of backward classes. The Commission submitted its report on 31st December 1980. The Commission estimated the population of Other Backward Classes at 52% based on 1931 Census data, and adopted eleven criteria to identify educationally and socially backward classes. The recommendations of the Second Backward Classes Commission (Mandal Report) were implemented by the Government on August 12, 1990 providing inter alia reservation of 27% to socially and educationally backward classes with effect from 7.8.1990 for the vacancies in Civil posts and services under Central Government filled through direct recruitment. The reservation rules were also applicable to Public Sector Undertakings, Financial Institutions, including banks, autonomous bodies, statutory and semi-government bodies and voluntary agencies receiving grant from the Government. Incidentally, the reservation in promotions for OBCs was not provided. The Government had also constituted a Committee under Justice R.P. Prasad on November 16, 1992 in pursuance of the Supreme Court Judgment in *Indra Sawhney and others versus Indian Union* (Writ Petition (Civil) No. 930 of 1990) to determine the criteria for identification of the socially advanced persons/sections for exclusion of creamy layer and the criteria recommended by the Committee has been accepted by the Government. Government of India vide DOP&T. O.M. No. 36012/22/93-Est, (SCT), dated 8.9.1993 provided reservation to socially and educationally backward classes as under:

(i) 27 per cent of vacancies in civil posts and services under the Government of India to be filled through direct recruitment, shall be reserved for the Other Backward Classes;

(ii) Candidates belonging to OBCs recruited on the basis of merit in an open competition on the same standards prescribed for the general candidates shall not be adjusted against the reservation quota of 27 percent;

(iii) The aforesaid reservation shall not apply to Other Backward Classes belonging to the creamy layer;

(iv) The OBCs for the purpose of the aforesaid reservation should compromise , the castes and communities which are common to both the lists in the report of the Mandal Commission and the State Governments' lists;

(v) The reservations provided to SCs, STs and OBCs put together do not exceed 50% of vacancies arising in an year;

(vi) No reservation for OBCS in promotion;

(vii) In respect of written examinations and interview, in order to fill the quota earmarked to OBCs relaxation of standards be provided to OBC candidates as in the case of SC/ST candidates;

(viii) Relaxation of marks for grant of Non-technical Scholarships/Book Awards to OBCS; and

(ix) Three years age relaxation would be given to the candidates of Other Backward Classes for direct recruitment over and above the prescribed age limit.

The above conditions were also applicable in matters of reservations for OBCs to autonomous bodies, statutory and semi-government bodies and voluntary agencies receiving grants from the Government. The reservation for Scheduled Castes and Scheduled Tribes is determined in proportion to the population of SCs and STs in the respective State/ UT but for OBCs it is fixed taking into account the proportion of their population in the concerned State/UT, subject to a maximum of 27% and the fact that the total reservation provided to SCs, STs and OBCs should not exceed the limit of 50%. Besides, the percentages of reservations provided in favour of SCs, STs and OBCs in matters of recruitment to group "C" & "D" under Central Government generally attracting local or regional talents vary from State to State subject to upper limit of 50% in aggregate. The details of the percentages of reservations fixed in the States are given below:

Table 2.1. Reservations In States/UTs

S. No.	*Name of the State / Union Territory*	*Percentage of Reservation*		
		SCs	*STs*	*OBCs*
01	Andhra Pradesh	16	7	27
02.	Arunachal Pradesh	1	45	0
03.	Assam	7	12	27
04.	Bihar	16	1	27
05.	Chhattisgarh	12	32	6
06.	Goa	2	0	18
07.	Gujarat	7	15	27
08.	Haryana	19	0	27
09.	Himachal Pradesh	25	4	20
10.	Jammu & Kashmir	8	11	27
11.	Jharkhand	12	26	12
12.	Karnataka	16	7	27
13.	Kerala	10	1	27
14.	Madhya Pradesh	15	20	15
15.	Maharashtra	10	9	27
16.	Manipur	3	34	13
17.	Meghalaya	1	44	5
18.	Mizoram	0	45	5
19.	Nagaland	0	45	0
20.	Orissa	16	22	12

S. No.	*Name of the State / Union Territory*	*Percentage of Reservation*		
21.	Punjab	29	0	21
22.	Rajasthan	17	13	20
23.	Sikkim	5	21	24
24.	Tamil Nadu	19	1	27
25.	Tripura	17	31	2
26.	Uttaranchal	18	3	13
27.	Uttar Pradesh	21	1	27
28 .	West Bengal	23	5	22
29.	Andaman & Nicobar Island	0	8	27
30.	Chandigarh	18	0	27
31.	Dadra & Nagar Haveli	2	43	5
32.	Daman & Diu	3	9	27
33.	Delhi	1	7.5	27
34.	Lakshadweep	0	45	0
35.	Pondicherry	16	0	27

Source: Table 8.4, GOI, DOP&T OM N.36017/1/2004-Est. (Res.) dated 5-7-2005. Misra Commission Report (p. 123)

The above Table 2.1 abundantly reveals that massive efforts have been made in the country to benefit the marginalized, backward and depressed sections of the society such as the SCs, STs and OBCs in the form of providing reservations in case of direct recruitment to group 'C ' &' 'D' under Central Government by reserving seats for them in all the States and Union Territories of the country.

The Constitution adopted a two–prong strategy to guarantee equality to the depressed, marginalized and backward classes. On the one side, it secured equality before the law in such a way that everyone irrespective of his caste, class, creed, colour, gender, religion or place of birth will receive equal protection of the law and be treated equally. On the other side, it empowered the State to make special provisions to promote the educational and economic interest of the SCs, STs, OBCs and minorities and to provide legal and other safeguards against discrimination in various spheres. For instance, Article 14- Right to equality provides equality before law and equal protection of laws by asking the State not to deny any person equality before the law or the equal protection of the laws within the territory of India. This Article providing equality of status and equal access to public resources and conveniences became an important ingredient of Fundamental Rights. Articles 15 and 16 of the Constitution prohibit the State from making any positive or negative discrimination on the grounds only of religion, race, caste, sex, decent, place of birth, residence or any of them or in matters pertaining to employment or appointment to any office under the State. Since the Supreme Court vide its decision in *State of Madras* versus *Smt. Champakam Dorairajan* (AIR 1951SC 525; 1951 SCR 525) had declared reservation of seats for various communities invalid on the basis of caste and religion, clause (4) was inserted under Article 15 to undo the effect of the decision of Supreme Court in the above mentioned case. Article 15(4) was added by amending Constitution(Ninety-third Amendment Act, 2005) to make any special provision for admission of any socially and educationally backward classes of citizens or the Scheduled Castes and Scheduled Tribes to educational institutions whether aided or unaided by the State, other than minority educational Institutions. Similarly, Clauses (1), (2) and (3) of Article 16 concerning equality of opportunity stipulate the rule of equality of opportunities in Public Employment and prohibit discrimination of any kind only on the grounds of religion, race, caste, sex, descent, place of birth, residence or any of them in matters of any employment or appointment under the State. In view of the presence of different segments of the people with different disabilities certain exceptions to the general law of equality were permitted. For instance, Article 16(4) states that "Nothing in this Article shall prevent the state from making any provision for the reservation of appointments or posts in favour of any backward class of citizens, which in the opinion of the State, is not adequately represented in the services under the State." Besides, Article 16 (4A) and Amendment Act, in 2001 were pursued to overcome the decision of Supreme Court in *Indra Sawhney versus Union of India*. Article 16(4A) empowers the State to make provisions for reservation in matters of promotion under the state in favour of SCs and STs which in the opinion of the State are not adequately represented in the services/ vacancies which were determined in accordance with clause (4) or (4A) of Article 16 by launching special drive. As the Article 335 imposes responsibility on the State to ensure the maintenance of efficiency of administration, a proviso to Article 335 was inserted by the Constitution 82nd Amendment Act, 2000 so as to overcome the problem arising after the decision of Supreme Court in *S. Vinod Kumar versus Union of India* which enables the State to make any provision in favour of SCs and STs for the relaxation of marks or lowering down of standards for reservation in promotions. Article 46 is also one of the most important Articles under Part IV of the Constitution (Directive Principles of State Policy). It promotes the educational and economic interests of SCs, STs and other weaker sections of the society by emphasizing that "the State shall promote with special care the educational and economic interests of weaker sections of the people and in particular of Scheduled Castes and Scheduled Tribes and shall protect them from social injustice & all forms of exploitation." Incidentally, the Constitution of India does not define "weaker sections of people" and the Supreme Court in the case of *Shantistar Builders versus Narayan Khimalal Tokame* directed the Central Government to suggest appropriate measures to clarify the expression "weaker sections of people". In Indra Sawhney's case the Supreme Court differentiated the phrase "Backward Class of citizens" as used in Article 16(4) and "Weaker sections of people" as mentioned in Article 46 and held that the expression "weaker sections of the people" was wider than the expression "Backward Class of citizens" or SEBCs or SCs or STs. It covers all sections of society who are rendered weak due to several circumstances such as poverty and natural and physical handicaps.

It is a fact that the Constitution of India does not provide any limit or specific percentage of reservation in favour of Scheduled Castes, Scheduled Tribes and Backward Classes but the successive decisions of the Supreme Court beginning with *Balaji v the State of Mysore* (1963) have fixed a general ceiling of 50% for all reservations taken together. Many jurists and Constitutional experts have expressed their reservations considering the 50% limit beneficial to the forward and privileged castes at the cost of marginalized and backward sections of the society. There are several agencies at the higher levels to regulate, monitor and implement reservation. For example, the Ministry of Social Justice and Empowerment, Ministry of Tribal Affairs and Planning Commission (Backward Caste Division) function as the nodal agencies for policy formulation, finalization and implementation of various educational, welfare and developmental programmes for SCs, STs and OBCs. Moreover, the Department of Personnel and Training (DOP&T) and Pensions, Government of India through administrative heads of Ministries and organizations regulate and monitor the reservation policy in public services at national level and enforces the rules and makes changes thereof whenever warranted and ensures the fulfillment of reserved quota. Furthermore, in each Ministry/Department and Government founded Organizations there are separate administrative units for Scheduled Castes, Scheduled Tribes and Other Backward Castes with liaison officers who are duty bound that all instructions issued by the Government on reservation for SCs,STs and OBCs are strictly complied with. Beside, there is a National Commission for Scheduled Castes set up under Article 338 of the Constitution as a High level Independent Constitutional body to investigate, evaluate and monitor all matters relating to safeguards provided for under the Constitution or under any other law for the time being in force or under any order of the Government and to monitor the impact of various developmental schemes and programmes on the growth and development of the Scheduled Castes. Likewise, the National Commission for Scheduled Tribes too was constituted under Article 338A of the Constitution as a high level independent Constitutional body to investigate, evaluate and monitor all matters pertaining to safeguards provided for under the Constitution or under any law or order of Government. Similarly, in pursuance of the direction of Supreme Court, the Government of India enacted the National Commission for Backward Classes Act 1993(Act No, 27 of 1993) and constituted a National Commission for Backward Classes at the Centre. Section 9(1) of the Act provides that it shall examine the requests for inclusion of any class of citizens as a backward class in the list and hear complaints of Over-Inclusion or Under-Inclusion of any backward class in such list and tender such advice to the Central Government as it deems appropriate. As per Section 9(2) of the Act such advice of the Commission shall generally be binding upon the Central Government and Section 11 provides for periodic revision of list by the Central Government.

The Impact of Reservation on Education and Employment of SCs/ STs and Backward Classes

We would now like to see the impact of these various measures upon the SCs, STs and the Backward Classes. The number of persons absorbed in the Central Government and the representation of Scheduled Castes and Scheduled Tribes and other Backward classes is provided in Table 2.2

From the above Table it is evident that the SCs/STs which were the most neglected castes and which had no presence in the governing structure prior to Independence marked their substantial presence in government sector approaching nearly their share in population of the country. Despite the fact that the employment opportunities from 1994 onward were declining perhaps due to abandoning the 1960s socialistic approach and the mounting expenditure of salaries, wages and pensions, consuming measure portion of the budget, the representation of Scheduled Castes and Scheduled Tribes went on increasing in percentage terms from 1974 to 2004, approaching nearly to their proportion in total population. Since, the reservations of Scheduled Castes and Scheduled Tribes were in effect since 1947 and 1950 respectively and the Other Backward Classes were provided reservation merely from 1993, the above Table does not provided a realistic picture about the participation of the Backward Classes in the Government jobs. We would, therefore, examine the Table 2.3 which shows group wise and total representation of Scheduled Castes, Scheduled Tribes and Other Backward Classes in percentage terms since 1965 in Central Government services.

From Table 2.3 it is abundantly visible that the share of Scheduled Castes and Scheduled Tribes in groups A, B, C and D during the last fifty years has continuously increased. In Central Services Groups A and B the representation of the Scheduled Castes has increased from merely 1.64% and 2.82% in 1965 to 12.20% and 14.50% in 2004 respectively. Likewise,

Table 2.2: Total Employment by the Central Government and Representation of SCs, STs & OBCs therein.

Year As on 1st of Jan.	*Total Employees in Central Government Services Including SC, ST and OBC's*	*Scheduled Castes*		*Scheduled Tribes*		*Other Backward Classes*	
		No. of Employees	*%*	*No. of Employees*	*%*	*No. of Employees*	*%*
1974	28,95,359	3,95,473	13.66	81,475	2.81		
1984	33,03,342	5,27,573	15.97	1,49,391	4.52		
1994	35,67,112	6,02,670	16.90	1,95,802	5.49		
1999	35,44,740	5,91,740	16.70	2,18,653	6.17		
2004	30,58,506	5,21,423	17.05	1,99,991	6.54	1,38,680	4.53

Source : Table 8.5, Tenth Five Year Plan, 2002-07, Volume II and DOP&T Note No.42011/24/2006-Estt, (Res.), dated 31.8.2006 (Misra Commission Report p. 124)

Table 2.3: Representation of the SCs, STs& OBCs in Central Government Services (%)

As on 1st ofJan	Group A			Group B			Group C			Group D			Total		
	SC	ST	OBC	SC	ST	BC	SC	ST	OBC	SC	ST	OBC	SC	ST	OBC
1965	1.64	0.27	,,	2.82	0.34	,,	8.88	1.14	,,	17.75	3.39	,,	13.17	2.25	,,
1970	2.36	0.40	,,	3.84	0.37	,,	9.27	1.47	,,	18.09	3.59	,,	13.09	2.4	,,
1975	3.43	0.62	,,	4.98	0.59	,,	10.71	2.27	,,	18.64	3.99	,,	13.84	2.94	,,
1980	4.95	1.06	,,	8.54	1.29	,,	13.44	3.16	,,	19.46	5.38	,,	15.67	3.99	,,
1985	7.3	1.73	,,	10.03	1.57	,,	14.87	4.2	,,	20.8	5.70	,,	16.83	4.66	,,
1990	8. 64	2.58	,,	11.29	2.39	,,	15.19	4.8 3	,,	21.46	6.73	,,	16.97	5.33	,,
1995	10.15	2.89	,,	12.67	2.68	,,	16.15	5.69	,,	21.26	6.48	,,	17.43	5.78	,,
2001	11.42	3.58	,,	12.82	3.70	,,	16.25	6.46	,,	17.89	6.81	,,	16.41	6.36	,,
2002	11.09	3.97	,,	14.08	4.18	,,	16.12	5.93	,,	20.07	7.13	,,	16.98	6.11	,,
2003	11.93	4.18	,,	14.32	4.32	,,	16.29	6.54	,,	17.98	6.96	,,	16.52	6.46	,,
2004	12.20	4.10	3.9	14.50	4.60	2.30	16.90	6.70	5.20	18.40	6.70	3.30	17.05	6.54	3.65

Source: :Table 8.6, DOP&T Vide their Note No.42.11/24/2006-Estt.(Res.) dated August 30th , 2006.(Misra Commission Report p. 125)

in Group C they have nearly doubled their strength during the last five decades from 8.88% in 1965 to 16.90% in 2004. Similarly, their representation in Group D and in total too has reached to the levels of 18.40% and 17.05% which is more than their proportion in the total population. In the same way, the Scheduled Tribes too increased their representations in Groups A and B from merely 0.27% and 0.34% in 1965 to 4.10% and 4.60% in 2004 respectively. In Group C also they made tremendous progress during the last fifty years for their share increased from 1.14% in 1965 to 6.70% in 2004. Moreover, in Group D and in the total also they progressed from 3.39% and 2.25% in 1965 to 6.70% and 6.54% in 2004 respectively approaching their proportion in total population. Since the data for Other Backward Classes is for 2004 only we cannot deduce any trend save this that their representation in employment in the Central Government during 2004 was merely 4.53% which was far less than their proportion in the population. However, looking to the data provided by Table 2.4 pertaining to All India Services like Indian Administrative Service, Indian Police Service, and Indian Foreign Service and Central Services Group A & B for which recruitment is made through Civil Services Examination of Union Public Service Commission, it is amply evident that the representation of Scheduled Castes, Scheduled Tribes and Other Backward classes is more or less equal to their share in the population of the country.

It is clear from the Table 2.4 that the representation of Scheduled Castes in IAS, IPS, IFS and Group A was to the extent of 13.1%, 12.5%, 5.0% and 19.0 respectively compared to 6.6%, 9.0%, 10% and 9.3 for Scheduled Tribes and 28.6%, 23.9%, 25.0% and 27% for OBCs. This shows that the share of Scheduled Castes was better compared to their proportion in IAS and IPS though slightly less in IFS. Similarly, the representation of Scheduled Tribes in IPS, IFS and Group A was more than their proportion in total population. As far as OBCs were concerned, their share was slightly better than their reserved quota among IAS category, equal to in Central Services but less in IPS, IFS and Central Services. Let us now examine Table 2.5 which shows the employment status of

Table 2.4: Representation of SCs, STs and OBCs in the All India and Central Services (Group A & B) through Civil Services Examination (%).

Year	*IAS*			*IPS*			*IFS*			*Central Services*			*Central Services*		
										Group A			*Group B*		
	SC	*ST*	*OBC*	*SC*	*ST*	*OBC*	*SC*	*ST*	*OBC*	*SC*	*ST*	*OBC*	*SC*	*ST*	*OBC*
2004	13.1	6.6	28.6	12.5	9.52	23.9	5.01	10.0	25.0	19.0	9.3	27.0	”	”	”

Source: Table 8.7, Misra Commission Report, p. 126.

Table 2.5: Representation of the SCs, STs and OBCs in 212 Public Enterprises as on 01.01. 2006

Category	*Total No. of Employees*	*Representation of SCS, STs and OBCs*					
		SCs		*STs*		*OBCs*	
		No.	*%*	*No.*	*%*	*No.*	*%*
Group A	1,65,405	20,864	12.61	6,607	3.99	10,410	6.29
Group B	1,54,174	20,335	13.18	9,44	6.12	13,001	8.43
Group C	6,64,501	1,31,204	19.74	84,957	9.77	1,13,407	17.06
Group D	2,42,973	53,027	21.82	34,594	14.23	54,845	22.57
(Excluding safai Karam-charis)							
Total	12,27,053	2,25,430	18.37	1,15,602	9.42	1,91,663	15.61

Source: Table 8.8, Annual Report of Department of Public Enterprises, 2005-06 (Misra Commission Report, p. 126.)

Scheduled Castes, Scheduled Tribes and Other Backward Classes and their representation in 212 Central Public Sector Undertakings.

As is manifest from the above Table that the representation of the Scheduled Castes in Central Government Enterprises was highly comfortable. In Group A and B their share was around 13% which was near to their proportion in total population while in Group C and Group D as well as in total they exceeded their proportion in total population. The same was the case with STs. Their representation in Group A was on the lower side but in group B it was nearer to their share while in Group C , D and total they too exceeded their proportion in total population. However, the OBCs were under represented in almost all the categories but their share compared to their reserved quota in Group A, B and in total was miserable. If we go into the details of employment status of Scheduled Castes and Scheduled Tribes in the Public Sector Banks and Insurance Sector as given in Table 2.6, we find that the Scheduled Castes are in dominant and comfortable position in almost all segments compared to Scheduled Tribes and Other Backward Classes.

The Table 2.6 conveys that among the categories of Officers, Clerks, Sub-staff, sweepers and the total, Scheduled Castes were above their share in total population.In the list of Sub-staff and sweepers they far exceed their proportion reaching to the level of 25.31% and 56.75% respectively. Though STs did not touch their share in total population but they were nearer to their proportion. Besides, compared to the OBCs they were far better represented in percentage terms in almost all segments. It is irony of fate that the OBCs were highly underrepresented in almost all the categories save Sub-staff where they were 22.55%, somewhat nearer to their reserved quota at 27%. It is however, quite strange that OBCs had 7.88% sweepers which is a new disclosure, for sweepers are mostly found in Scheduled Castes and Scheduled Tribes but not in OBCs. It appears that some marginalized and depressed OBC lads might have joined as sweepers under compulsion of getting jobs in order to meet their two ends. The figures regarding the representation of SCs and STs in Insurance

Table 2.6: Representation of SCs, and STs and Other Backward Classes in Public Sector Banks and Financial Institutions on 31.12.2005

Category	*Total No. of Employees*	*No. of Employees belonging to*					
		SCs		*STs*		*OBCs*	
		No.	*%*	*No.*	*%*	*No.*	*%*
Officers	2,58,543	40,076	15.50	14,186	5.49	6,570	2.54
Clerks	3,44,426	55,776	16.10	17,114	4.97	11,436	3.32
Sub-staff	1,48,343	37,550	25.31	9,896	6.67	33,453	22.55
Sweepers	39,784	22,576	56.75	2,496	6.27	3,136	7.88
Total	7,91,096	1,55,978	19.72	43,690	5.52	54,595	6.90

Source: Table 8.9, Department of Economic Affairs, Banking division Note No. 5/10/2006-SCT (B) dt. 4th December, 2006.(Misra Commission Report, p. 127)

Sector reveal that the performance of SCs and STs is not bad. The Table 2.7 shows the representation of SCs and STs in the Insurance Sector as on 1.1.2002.

The Table 2.7 exhibits that the share of SCs in Group A was more than their share in total population in all companies

Table 2.7: Representation of SCs and STs in the Insurance Sector as on 1.1. 2002.

Company / Group	*Total Employees*	*S.C. Employees*	*Percentage of S.Cs*	*S.T. Employees*	*Percentage of S.T. Employees*
Group A					
National	3919	602	15.36	108	2.75
New India	5041	784	15.52	155	3.07
Oriental	4049	676	16.69	103	2.54
United India	4695	880	18.74	155	3.30
GIC	322	38	11.80	11	3.40
LIC	17023	2692	15.81	896	5.26
Total	35049	5672	16.18	1428	4.07
Group B					
National	2670	241	9.02	46	1.72
New India	3732	365	9.78	105	2.81
Oriental	2814	323	11.36	89	3.13
United India	2851	275	9.60	56	1.96
GIC	0	0	0	0	0
LIC	19079	2662	13.95	891	4.67
Total	31146	3866	12.41	1187	3.81

Company / Group	*Total Empl-oyees*	*S.C. Empl-oyees*	*Percentage of S.Cs*	*S.T. Empl-oyees*	*Perc-entage of S.T. Empl-oyees*
Group C					
National	10018	2007	20.03	529	5.28
New India	12001	2039	16.89	492	4.07
Oriental	9667	1824	18.97	588	6.08
United India	10908	2356	21.59	617	5.66
GIC	263	68	25.86	13	4.94
LIC	74414	12518	16.82	5628	7.56
Total	117271	20812	17.74	7867	6.70
Group D					
(Excluding Sweepers)					
National	1824	606	33.22	122	6.68
New India	2599	1007	38.74	231	8.88
Oriental	1936	609	31.15	160	8.26
United India	2423	1009	41.64	188	7.75
United India	2423	1009	41.64	188	7.75
GIC	95	26	27.37	13	16.38
LIC	8277	2090	25.25	688	8.31
Total	17154	5347	31.17	1402	8.17

Note: There is no provision of Group B in GIC of India.

Source: Table 8.10, 7th Report of the National Commission for Scheduled Castes and Scheduled Tribes 2001-2002. (Misra Commission Report p. 128)

save GIC but the STs lagged behind in all Insurance companies. In Group B both the SCs and STs lagged behind and could not touch their share. As against this, in Group C the Scheduled Castes remained comfortable as they achieved beyond their share in all Insurance companies. However, the STs lagged behind save in LIC where they touched their 7.5% mark. In Group D the position for both the castes was favorable as the SCs were represented on an average in all the companies to the extent of 31.17% compared to their reserved quota of 15%. Likewise, the STs lagged behind only with reference to National where their share was 6.68% but save this they too achieved on an average 8.17% in all companies compared to their quota of 7.5%. The Employment status of the Scheduled Castes and Scheduled Tribes in Indian Railways during 2004-05 is shown in the Table 2.8.

As is visible from Table 2.8, the representation of Scheduled Castes in Group A and C was more or less equal to their quota. However, it was on the higher sides in Group B and D as well as in the total being 16.20%, 19.22% and 16.52% respectively. As against this, the representation of STs too was not bad. It was more or less equal to their quota among Groups A, B, C, D and the total. The representation of the Scheduled Castes, Scheduled Tribes and Other Backward Classes as shown in Table 2.9 was remarkable in other sectors of economy such as Services, Agriculture and Production.

From the Table 2.9 it is clear that the representation of Scheduled Castes and Scheduled Tribes was far more than their reservation quota in services, agriculture and production. In Professional and Managerial jobs as well as in sales their share was slightly below their combined quota of 22.5%. It was, however, heartening to know that they occupied 30.7% of the total jobs nearly 8.2% more than their reserved quota. Likewise, the OBCs too captured more jobs than their 27% quota in sales, services, agriculture, production and total jobs. Their share in professional and managerial cadre was slightly less than their reserved quota. The interesting thing is that the share of SCs/STs and OBCs in services, agriculture, production and the total jobs was higher than that of Hindus. The most depressing aspect is the job position of the Muslims.

Table 2.8: Representation of SCs & STs in Railways

Group	*Number of Employees*	*Scheduled Castes*		*Scheduled Tribes*	
		Number of Employees	*Percentage to Total Employees in the Group*	*Number of Employee*	*Percentage to Total Employees in the Group*
Group A	8002	1,284	15.93	577	7.16
Group B	6686	1,094	16.20	404	5.98
Group C	872120	1,30,253	14.89	52,298	5.98
Group D	535443	1,02,925	19.22	34,619	6.46
Grand Total	14,22,251	2,35,556	16.52	87,898	6.16

Source: Table 8.11, Report of the National Commission for Railways and Linguistic Minorities (Misra Commission Report p.128).

Table 2.9: Representation of OBCs in different Sectors of Economy

Category of Jobs	*SC/ST*	*Muslims*	*OBC*	*Hindus*
1. Professional and Managerial	14.3	9.7	24.2	51.8
2. Sales	15.5	14.7	28.2	41.5
3. Services	28.6	9.1	36.5	25.8
4. Agriculture	36.3	6.1	35.7	21.9
5. Production	28.8	16.6	33.3	21.2
6. Total of Jobs	30.7	9.5	33.7	26.1

Source: Table 8.12, Report on Reservation Workshop by JNU based on NSSO Report 1999-2000. (Misra Commission Report p. 129).

Despite the fact that Muslims occupied a prominent position among all the sectors of economy in pre-partition days and presently they touch nearly the 15% mark in India's population which is more or less equal to Scheduled Castes their share is the lowest among all sectors. They are behind Scheduled Castes and Scheduled Tribes, Other Backward Castes and Hindus. In professional and managerial areas where they were renowned, their share is merely 9.7% compared to14.3% for SCs/STs, 24.2% for OBCs and 51.8% for Hindus. Similarly, in sales they are 14.7% compared to 15.5%, 28.2% and 41.5% SCs/STs, OBCs and Hindus respectively. Likewise, in services where they should have been more, they were merely 9.1% as against 28.6% SCs/STs, 36.5% OBCs and 25.8% Hindus. In the same way, in agriculture their share was just 6.1% as contrasted to 36.3% for SCs/STs, 35.7% OBCs and 21.9% Hindus. Moreover, in production they occupied only 16.6% jobs in comparison to 28.8% for SCs/STs, 33.3% for OBCs and 21.2% Hindus. The most frustrating aspect was their share in total jobs which was only 9.5% as against 30.7% for SCs/STs, 33.7% for OBCs and 26.1% for Hindus.

As far as the engagement of SCs, STs and OBCs in organized and unorganized private sectors is concerned, the complete details about their engagement is not available. It is claimed that the organized private sector and the Government sector employ very little segment of the work force of the country. The organized private sector employed about 84.32 lakh persons in 2002, mostly in manufacturing and community and social service which was less than 3% of the total work force numbering nearly 350 million. According to survey conducted by the Central Statistical Organization (CSO) in 1998, covering 30.35 million enterprises in the country other than crop production and plantations, 80% or 24.39 million were self-financed. Among them 44.8% enterprises in rural and urban areas were owned by the SCs, STs and OBCs as per Table 2.10.

Table 2.10: Ownership of the Enterprises by SCs, STs & OBCs (%)

	Rural	*Urban*	*Combined*
Scheduled Castes	9.0	5.8	7.7
Scheduled Tribes	5.2	2.3	4.0
Other Backward Classes	36.0	29.1	33.1
Total	50.2	37.2	44.8

Source: Table 8.19, Reservation and Private Sector (Edition 2005) by Sukhdeo Thorat (Misra Commission Report p. 134).

Table 2.10 manifests that the ownership of enterprises owned by the Scheduled Castes reached to the level of 7% in rural and urban areas taken together. Compared to urban sector their ownership was larger in rural areas similarly, the STs also fared equally well. Their share in the ownership of enterprises was around 7% in urban and rural areas but compared to the rural areas (4.0%) their share too was less in urban areas. However, the ownership of enterprises for the Other Backward Classes exceeded their reserved quota in the rural as well as urban segments. They had their more or less equal presence in rural and urban areas. The above facts can be appreciated only when they are perceived in the context of pre-Independence period when the SCs and STs could hardly think of owning significant portion of self-financing enterprises.

Educational Position Of Scheduled Castes and Scheduled Tribes

Let us examine the literacy and educational status of the Scheduled Castes and Scheduled Tribes in order to see the impact of reservation upon these communities. The Table 2.11 shows enrolment status of SCs and STs between 1980-81 and 2003-04.

Table 2.11: Comparative Enrolment Status of Scheduled Castes and Scheduled Tribes (1980-81 – 2003-04)

(figure in thousands)

Year	*Total Enrol-ment*	*SC. Enrol-ment*	*% of SC Enrol-ment*	*ST Enrol-ment*	*% of ST Enro-lment*
1980-81	72688	10981	15.11	4660	6.41
1985-86	86465	13921	16.10	6580	7.61
1990-91	99119	15794	16.93	7869	7.94
1995-96	109734	185 36	16.89	9224	8.40
1999-2000	113612	204 435	17.98	10650	9.37
2000-2001	113800	21195	18.62	10995	9.66
2001-2002	113883	21504	18.88	11731	10.30
2002-2003	122 397	21669	17.70	11830	9.67
2003-2004	128266	23129	18.04	12517	9.75

Source: Table 8.14, Selected Educational Statistics of Ministry of HRD for the year 2003-04 (Misra Commission Report p. 131).

The above Table reveals that the enrolment position of the Scheduled Caste candidates remained quite favourable as they crossed their share in reserved quota between 1980-81 and 2003-04. Likewise, the ST candidates too did not remain

Table 2.12: Comparative Educational Status of Religious Communities at different levels.

(In percentage)

Religious/ Communities	*Up to Primary*	*Middle-*	*Seco ndary*	*Senior Secondary*	*Diploma*	*Graduation*	*Unclassified*
All Religion	55.57	16.09	14.13	6.74	0.72	6.72	0.02
Hindus	54.91	16.18	14.25	6.92	0.71	7.01	0.01
Muslims	65.31	15.14	10.96	4.53	0.41	3.6	0.05
Christians	45.79	17.13	17.48	8.7	2 .19	8.71	0.01
Sikhs	46.70	16.93	20.94	7.57	0.90	6.94	0.02
Buddhists	54.69	17.52	14.09	7.65	0.35	5.7	0.01
Jains	29.51	12.27	21.87	13.84	1.03	21.47	0.01
Other Religions	62.12	17.48	11.24	4.55	0.26	4.35	0.01

Source: Table 8.15, Census of India 2001 (Misra Commission Report p. 131).

Table 2.13: Scheduled Castes and Scheduled Tribes Studying at different Level of Education

Level of Education	*Total*	*General*		*SC*		*ST*	
		No.	*%*	*No.*	*%*	*No.*	*%*
Ph.D.	65525	60282	92.0	3859	5.9	1384	2.1
M.A.	427234	354675	83.0	58017	13.6	14542	3.4
M.Sc.	237439	207470	87.4	29484	10.5	4985	2.1
M,Com.	141954	124378	87.6	14119	10.0	3457	2.4
BA/BA Hons.	3824833	3107202	81.3	513771	13.4	203860	5.3
B.SC./B.Sc.Hons	1614067	1399426	86.7	178829	11.1	35812	2.2.
B.Com Hons	1613374	1432000	88.8	150616	9.3	30758	1.9
BE/B.SC Engg/B.Arch	772923	708782	91.7	48783	6.3	15358	2.0
Medical/Dental/ Nursing/Pharmacy/ Ayurveda	223235	184194	82.5	28935	13.0	10106	4.6
B.Ed./BT	114681	90298	78.7	18023	15.7	6360	5.6
Other	973873	738435	75.8	153094	15.7	82344	8.5

Source: Table 8.16, Selected Educational Statistics 2003-04 (Misra Commission Report p. 132).

behind as they also over reached their proportion in total population in matters of enrolment between 1980-81 and 2003-04. The comparative educational status of religious communities at different levels reveals as per table 2.12 that save up to Primary level, Muslims lagged behind at all levels in contrast to All religions, Hindus, Christians, Sikhs, Buddhists, Jains and other religions.

The condition of Muslims among all the segments of the society seems to be miserable for save at Upper Primary level they are far behind at the level of Middle, Secondary, Senior Secondary, Diploma, graduation and unclassified category compared to All Religions, Hindus, Christians, Sikhs, Buddhists, Jains and Other Religions. Not only this, their percentages went on decreasing from 65.31% in Upper Primary level to 15.14% in Middle, 10.96 in Secondary, 4.53% in Senior Secondary, 0.41% in Diploma,3.6% in graduation and 0.05% in unclassified segment. Besides, they were far below national average at all levels except Upper Primary level. As against this, Hindus, Christians, Sikhs Buddhists and Jains were generally better off almost at all levels compared to national averages. If we now look towards the picture pertaining to the representation of Scheduled Castes and Scheduled Tribes in higher education, we find that they have made progress practically in every field though their percentage is somewhat lower than their reserved quota which is visible from Table 2.13

The Table 2.13 shows that the Scheduled Tribes have shown their presence in almost all areas of higher education including PhD, Engineering, B.Ed. medical and others but their representation is not up to their proportion in total population. Likewise, the Scheduled Castes despite their all round progress in all the segments of higher education have not touched their reserved quota save in B.Ed./BT and others. In M.A and BA/BA Hons. as well as Medical/Dental/Nursing/ Ayurvedic they have reached to the extent of 13.6%, 13.4% and 13% respectively. Similarly, they are nearly 10% or above in B.Com .Hons. and M.Sc. as well as M.Com. and B.SC/ B.Sc.,Hons

From the facts and figures given in support of educational development and the employment position of the Scheduled

Castes, Scheduled Tribes and the Other Backward Castes, it is amply clear that the policy of reservation had a salutary effect upon the growth and development of these castes and classes. It is heartening to note that the Scheduled Castes and the Scheduled Tribes have come within the main stream though they were considered not only as untouchables but also more or less the out-castes till 1947. They were so exploited, marginalized and backward that they could not think of having pacca houses, getting jobs in any respectable profession, wearing gold and silver and sending their children to schools. Socially, economically, culturally and politically they were the lowest part of the society. No part of the society could have social and cultural relations with them. Not only this, the doors of religious places were closed for them, they could not quench their thirst from the public taps, buy from the shops as normal customers and move about in public transport system with grace and dignity. Thanks to Dr. B.R. Ambedkar and the social reformers like him as well as the Indian Constitution and the sagacity of Indian people that they were provided reservations and other privileges at the Central and State levels as a consequence of which they are out of the rut under which they had to live for centuries. In modern India they have occupied important positions in legislature, judiciary, executive, army and media. Their members have enjoyed the privileges of the President of India, Chief Justice of the Supreme Court, Chief Ministers of States, ministers in the Central and State Governments, governors, ambassadors, secretaries, Vice-Chancellors and members of highest boards. They are found in each and every sector of the Central and State Governments. Though they have achieved a lot, their share in some of the categories in government sectors and some of the areas in higher education is not up to their reserved quota. In Group C and D they have exceeded their 15% and 7.5% quota but fall short here and there in group A and B. Unfortunately we could not get enough material pertaining to the educational and employment status of Other Backward Classes through Justice Ranganath Misra Report but whatever statistics we have about All India and Central Services where recruitment is made through Union Public Service Commission, the indications are that the Other Backward Classes too are nearer to their share.

Swaminathan S.A. Aiyar in his article in *Times of India* dated July 31, 2011 entitled "The unexpected rise of Dalit millionaires" has revealed that for centuries the dalit had been at the bottom of the income and social ladders, despised and exploited but due to their empowerment, they have now established a Dalit Chamber of Commerce and Industry in Mumbai. He stated that many people like Bhagwan Gawai, Sushil Patil, Ashok Khade and Balu who were just ordinary people have multiplied their wealth and presently they are rolling in money and wealth. A seminal study by Devesh Kapur and others revealed that the proportion of dalits owning their own business went up from 6% to 36.7% in Western UP. And from 4.2% to 11% in Eastern UP. Likewise the proportion in non-traditional occupations such as tailors, masons, etc. was up from 14% to 37% in the Eastern and from 9.3% to 42% in Western UP. The practice of being locked as *halwaha* or bonded labour is no more amongst them since *halwaha* proportion has declined from 32.1% to 1.1%. Similarly, the proportion of dalits doing farm work too has decreased from 76.0% to 45.6% in the East and from 46.1% to 20.5% in the West. In the same way their dependence upon their own lands has increased from 16.6% to 28.4% in the Eastern and from 50.5% to 67.6% in the Western UP. All this happened due to reservation, opportunities provided by the globalization and the empowerment drive by the Dalit Chief Minister in UP.

General Doubts about Pursuing the Reservation Policy

There are several conjectures, hunches and doubts raised by many Indians about the implementation of the reservation policy for SCs, STs and the OBCs. It is often alleged that the inefficiency, slackness and incompetence has entered into the governing structure as a matter of reservation since the persons who are admitted in various courses and appointed to various positions do not fulfill the required standards. Since they lack competence compared to their counterparts, they not only suffer due to inferiority complex but also hesitate to act independently which causes immense damage to the overall social, political, economic and administrative structure of the country. As against this, it is emphasized by the pro-reservation lobby that the advantages of giving reservation to the depressed sections far exceed the short term anomalies. Besides, it has been rightly said that situations and circumstance are the greatest teachers. Once a person gets a chance, he learns by his peers, trial and error and experience and sooner becomes a useful part of the society. Moreover, if there are certain short run weaknesses, they can be removed over time by training. It is also stated that the reservation policy has benefitted certain dominant segments within the reserved category and those who are less vocal, weak or marginalized failed to get any meaningful benefit out of it. For instance, Chamars in Uttar Pradesh and Mahars in Maharashtra are supposed to have benefitted most from reservation compared to other members of the Scheduled Castes. Similarly, the Meena community from among the Scheduled Tribes is believed to be highest beneficiary at the cost of other tribes. In Punjab the Valmiki Samaj is asking for a separate quota for them as they believe that Ramadasis and Mazbis have cornered their quota in favour of them. Likewise, it is alleged that among the Other Backward Classes the Ezhavas of Kerala, Nadars and Thevars of Tamil Nadu, Vokkalligas and Lingayats of Karnataka, Lods and Koeris of Central India, Yadavas and Kurmis in Bihar and UP and Jats in Rajasthan have benefitted most from reservation and other sections of backward classes have gained the least. Besides, many unscrupulous sections of the society have taken the advantage of reservation by obtaining the false certificates. The problem of false and fake caste or community certificates debar genuine people from the privileges of reservation. The Supreme Court too has expressed its displeasure and felt the need of a comprehensive policy to isolate the undesirable elements from getting the benefit of reservations. It is also said that reservation as a policy to up lift the backward castes and classes was adopted as a short term and temporary measure limited in duration for specific categories of people but as the time is elapsing, the bogy of reservation is acquiring added strength even from the sides of higher and privileged castes and classes. It is claimed by the eminent people of the society that the policy of reservation must be consistent with the policy of reservation which was adopted in the country at the initial stages and the vested interests should not be allowed to get the benefit of reservation perpetually. Once equality is achieved there should be no need of reservation or of any preferential treatment. The concept of reservation, in the opinion of many, is an exception to be used under exceptional circumstances merely to uplift the unequal to the level of equality as early as possible and not to perpetuate the inequality by making the equal unequal by providing crutches to equals. There are people who are demanding that those Castes and Classes which have achieved their reserved quota in admissions and appointments should be included in the list of developed castes or classes and reservations to them should be stopped forthwith. If this is not done then at least those who have reached the creamy layer of the society by coming out of the category of depressed and backward classes due to obtaining the benefits of reservation should be excluded from the privileges of reservation. Their wards who are competent enough to compete with other segments of the society in open competition should not be given any benefit of reservation. The need of the hour, therefore, is that the creamy layer which has been excluded from the list of Other Backward Classes should also be excluded from the list of Scheduled Castes and Scheduled Tribes. There is no dearth of people who are emphasizing that caste and religion should not be the basis of reservation. Ideally the criteria of reservation in the long run should be based on educational, social and economic backwardness and not religion or caste. Besides, the reservation on the basis of Article 16(4) only as a short term, time-bound and temporary measure should be provided to all those socially and economically weaker sections of the society including the minorities which have lagged behind in the process of growth and development so that they may participate as equals in the national reconstruction and mainstream.

3

The Educational and Economic Conditions of Muslims *vis-à-vis* Others at National Level

Minorities are basically a smaller segment or a part representing less than half of the whole in the context of the predominant section of the country, differing in race, religion, traditions, culture, language, script or political persuasion, possessing a wish to preserve their unique characteristics markedly different from those of the rest of population. In India since 80% people profess Hindu religion hence all those who profess other than Hindu religion are called minorities. The population of Religious Communities as per Census 2001 was as follows:

S. No.	*Types*	*In lakhs*	*Percentage*
1.	Total	10286.07	100
2.	Hindus	8275.78	80.5
3.	Muslims	1381.88	13.4
4.	Christians	240.80	2.3
5.	Sikhs	192.15	1.9
6	Buddhists	79.55	0.8
7.	Jains	42.25	0.4
8.	Others	66.39	0.6
9	Religion not stated	7.27	0.1

Muslims are a minority in the context of the Hindu majority but in themselves they are the largest segment of Muslims in the world perhaps next to Indonesia, Pakistan and Bangladesh and larger than many countries of Europe, Asia and Africa. According to 2001 Census they were13.4% of the total population or over 138 million out of 1028.6 million Indians. Presently they are nearly 150 million and many unofficial estimates put them in the range of 20% of the total population. Among Muslims it was found that during 2004-05 merely 0.8% were Scheduled Castes, 0.5% Scheduled Tribes, 39.2% Backward Castes and 59.5% Higher Castes. As per 2001 Census, 25.2% Muslims or 20.24 million lived in West Bengal, 24.7% or 7.86 million in Kerala, 18.5% or 30.74 million in Uttar Pradesh, 15.9% or 17.45 million in Bihar including Jharkhand, 30.9% or 8.24 million in Assam, 67.0% or 6.79 million in Jammu & Kashmir, 12.2% or 6.46 million in Karnataka, 11.7% or 1.6 million in Delhi, 10.6% or 10.27 million in Maharashtra, 9.2% or 6.99% million in Andhra Pradesh, 9.1% or 4.59 million in Gujarat, 8.5% or 4.79 million in Rajasthan, 5.2% or 4.25 million in Madhya Pradesh, 5.8% or 1.22 million in Haryana, 5.6% or 3.47 million in Tamil Nadu, 2.1% or 0.76 million in Orissa, 3.5% or 1.64 million in Punjab, Haryana and Chandigarh, 11.9% or 1.01 million in Uttaranchal, 2.0% or 0.41 million in Chattisgarh, 1.6% or 0.38 million in Punjab, In the same way, as per Census 2001 there were 13 districts in Uttar Pradesh, 12 in West Bengal, 8 in Bihar, 4 in Jammu & Kashmir, 3 in Maharashtra, 3 in Assam and one district each in Andhra Pradesh, Gujarat and Karnataka where Muslim population ranged between 30 % to 98%. Likewise, Apart from these fifty highly Muslim concentrated districts, there were 70 districts where Muslim population varied between 40 lakhs to five lakhs.

General Perceptions of Muslims

Muslims of India often lament that in spite of their brilliant historical past and significant number they are labouring under heavy odds. Almost all the segments of the society including the most backward and marginalized and depressed sections have been benefitted by the multidimensional and multifarious growth of the country but unfortunately they are at receiving end. The country and the people of India have made tremendous progress in all spheres and the prosperity of Indians is reflected in their living standards and ways of living but Muslims are drifting day by day in the vacuum created by the vertical growth of the centuries old depressed castes. India too is marching towards becoming the world power but Muslims have been struggling under the growth-shadow areas. Though a wide variety of welfare measures have been taken by the government but general perception among Muslims is that they are merely cosmetic in nature as all is not well with them. The process of accelerated growth in the country has not narrowed down the inequalities between them and the rest, but it has widened the development deficit between them and others. Muslims live with a sense of inferiority complex and the perception of being neglected or discriminated has paralyzed a large segment of Muslims resulting in their alienation. They have been deprived of their means of livelihood due to displacement of traditional occupations and are facing the brunt of competition unleashed by the globalization and liberalization. All pronouncements of Muslims may not be right but their charges of unfair treatment have some degree of truth which gives them added strength to assert with more force and conviction that all is not well with them and thus the situation continues to deteriorate perpetually. Rather than involving in blame game, the need of the hour is to go in to the root cause of deprivation of Muslims with a purpose of solving their problems by adopting affirmative, positive and bold initiatives. The acid test of any democratic, secular and vibrant State lies in its being considerate, helpful and friendly to its minorities. Inadvertently the Indian State has given the impression that it is under the duress from the side of the rightist parties and its lack of necessary will due to prevailing circumstances and the knee-jerk reaction have done more harm than good to Muslims. Moreover, a large section of the civil society and the meaningful people of the country too remained dormant under the hypnotism of ideologies and emotional issues with the result that the adversaries of Muslim community got free hand and Muslims were brought from bad to worse.

Educational and Economic Conditions of Muslim Community vis-à-vis Others

If we now analyze the educational and economic conditions of Muslims vis-à-vis other segments of the society especially the Backward Classes and Scheduled Castes and Scheduled Tribes, we find that they are at the bottom of the pyramid. The literacy among Muslims during 2001 as per Census 2001 was 59.1% compared to 65.1% among Hindus, 52.2% in SCs/STs, and 70.8% for all others. Likewise, in urban areas it was 70% as against 81% among Hindus, 68% SCs/STs and 85% all others. Similarly, in rural areas it was 53% in contrast to59% for Hindus, 49% for SCs/STs and 64% for all others. Moreover, for urban males and urban females it was 76% and 63% respectively as against 88% and 74% for Hindus, 78% and 58% for SCs/STs and 90% and 78% for all other urban males and females respectively. Likewise, for rural Muslim males and females it was 62% and 43% respectively compared to 72% and 46% for Hindus, 61% and 36% for SCs/STs and 77% and 52% all other rural males and females respectively. Thus, we find that compared to SCs/STs they were marginally better but they were far behind all other segments of Indian society.

Table 3.1: Literates as proportion of population by Age Groups-2004-05

Age Groups	*Hindus*			*Muslims*	*Other Minorities*
	Gen	*OBC*	*SCs/STs*		
6-13 Years	90.2	80.8	74.7	74.6	88.5
14-15 Years	95.7	87.5	80.0	79.5	91.9
16-17 Years	95.0	85.2	78.6	75.5	91.3
18-22 Years	91.4	76.9	65.0	70.5	85.8
23 years and above	74.0	50.6	36.5	46.1	67.0
Total	80.5	63.4	52.7	59.9	75.2

Source: Table 4.1, of Sachar Committee Report.

Table 3.1 of Sachar Committee Report shows proportion of literacy among different age groups during 2004-05.

From the Table 3.1 it is clear that General Hindus, OBC Hindus and other minorities were far better in matters of literacy in almost all age groups compared to Muslims. Muslims were far behind the SCs/STs in age groups 6-13, 14-15 and 16-17 because new generation of SCs/STs is increasingly acquiring education but Muslim children are reverting back to petty jobs to supplement the family income. However, within age groups 18-22 and 23 years and above Muslims were slightly better off compared to SCs/STs. If we look at percentage of people who completed at least Primary School during 2001, we find that 60.9% Muslims did it compared to 61.4% SCs/STs and 79.3% all others. Similarly, 40.5% Muslims completed at least Middle School in contrast to 41.3% SCs/STs and 62.7% all others. Likewise, 23.9% Muslims completed at least Matric as against 21.1% SCs/STs and 42.5% all others. When we compare the levels of literacy between Muslim OBCs and Hindu OBCs in the light of the following table, we notice marked differences:

Table 3.2. Literacy Levels of SRCs by Place of Residence

SRCs	*India*	*Urban*	*Rural*
Hindu OBCs	65.7	80.8	61.7
Muslim OBCs	61.9	70.1	57.8
India	67.3	82.6	61.9

Source: Table 10.4, Sachar Committee Report.

It is quite clear from the above figures that Muslim OBCs were not only behind the Hindu OBCs in urban, rural and at all India levels but they were far behind the national averages both at the urban and rural as well as all India planes. If we look at Table 3.3 (Sachar Committee Report) pertaining to the number of Muslim graduates and diploma and certificate holders as per Census 2001 figures compared to SCs/STs and others, we find a miserable picture.

Table 3.3: Graduates and Diploma Holders by SRCs

SRCs	*Number (In Lakhs)*		*Percentage of 20 Years + population*		*Distribution across SRCs*	
	Graduates	*Diploma and Certificate*	*Graduates*	*Diploma and Certificate*	*Graduates*	*Diploma and Certificate*
Total	376.7	40.5	6.7	0.7	100	100
Muslim	23.9	2.7	3.6	0.4	6.8	6.8
SCs/STs	30.8	4.1	2.4	0 3	8.2	10.2
All others	322	33.7	8.8	0.9	85.5	83.0

Source: Table 4.2, Sachar Committee Report.

The above figures show that out of 376.7 lakh graduates there were merely 23.9 lakh graduates among Muslims compared to 30.8 lakhs among SCs/STs, 322 lakh among all others. Similarly out of 40.5 lakh diploma and certificate holders Muslims were 2.7 lakhs in contrast to 2.7 lakh SCs/STs and 33.7 lakh all others. Muslims' percentage of graduates and diploma and certificate holders among 20 years + population was 3.6 and 0.4 compared to 2.4 and 0.3 for SCs/STs and 8.8 and 0.9 for all others respectively. Likewise, the distribution of the Muslim graduates and diploma and certificate holders across various socio-religious communities was 6.3 and 6.8 compared to 8.2 and 10.2 for SCs/STs and 85.5 and 83.0 for all others respectively. This again shows that in matters of acquiring graduation degrees and diplomas and certificates Muslims were nowhere. They were far behind

Table 3.4: Proportion of Persons aged 20 years + with Higher Education in each SRCs

SRCS	*General Graduates*	*Technical Graduates*	*Tech Dip / Cert.*	*Higher Education*
H-OBC	3.7	0.2	2.3	6.2
M-OBCs	2.3	0.1	1.7	4.1
Total	5.5	0.3	2.6	8.5

Source: Table 10.6 Sachar Committee Report

all other communities though they were slightly better off compared to the SCs/STs. Similarly, as per Table 3.4, Muslim OBCs too were lagging behind Hindu OBCs in matters of general, technical and higher education.

The statistics in Table 3.4 reveal that Muslim OBCs were not only far behind the Hindu OBCs in the areas pertaining to general and technical graduates as well as Technical Diplomas and Certificates but also in Higher education. They stood nowhere in comparison to all India level in these segments.

Employment Situation in Gainfull Activities

We know that a man's social prestige, cultural norms and economic standards are determined by the nature and quantum of his employment in gainful activities. If he is engaged as an important entrepreneur in industry, trade and commerce or absorbed in government jobs at higher level, he acquires respect and dignity and enjoys the comforts and luxuries of life. However, if he is engaged as a casual labourer in seasonal activities it becomes difficult for him even to meet the two ends. When we look at the engagement aspects of Muslims in gainful and useful activities, we observe that a relatively higher share of Muslims is engaged in self employment, manufacturing and trade activities. This is particularly true for Muslim women as well as Muslim urban workers. Besides, their participation in regular salaried jobs and government and salaried jobs in the public and private sectors is on the lower side compared to other segments of the society. They have no job security and are more vulnerable in terms of conditions of work since most of them are absorbed in the informal sector of the economy. In urban areas the probability of Muslim males and females getting regular jobs is lowest while that of SC/ST males and females getting such jobs is the highest. Likewise, in rural areas the probability of a SC and ST male worker getting non-agricultural job is higher compared to that of a Muslim male worker. The Table 3.5 (Sachar Committee Report) shows the distribution of workers in each religious group by activity:

Table 3.5: Distribution of Workers in Each Socio-Religious Category by Activity, Status and Place of Residence-2004-05, All Workers (Principal and Subsidiary, aged 15-64)

Activity Status	*Hindus*				*Muslims*	*Other Minorities*	
	All Hindus	*SCs/STs*	*OBCs*	*UC*			
Urban							
Own account worker in household enterprise	29.7	25	30.9	30.8	39.4	26.9	30.9
Employer in household Enterprise	2.3	0.6	1.7	3.7	2.0	4.2	2.4
Unpaid family worker in Household enterprise	10.6	7.3	13.5	9.5	15.9	10.1	11.3
Regular wage/salaried	42.3	39.9	36.4	49.3	27.0	44.7	40.3
Casual in public work	0.1	0.2	0.1	0.1	0.2	0.1	0.1
Casual in other work	15.0	26.6	17.4	6.7	15,5	13.9	15.0.
Total	100	100	100	100	100	100	100

Source: Table 5.4, Sachar Committee Report.

Table 3.5 (contd.)

Activity Status	*Hindus*				*Muslims*	*Other Minorities*	
	All Hindus	*SCs/STs*	*OBCs*	*UC*			
Rural							
Own account worker in Household enterprise	29.6	22.5	31.6	37.6	39.4	32.9	30.6
Employer in household Enterprise	0.8	0.2	0.8	1.8	1.0	1.9	0.9
Unpaid family worker in household enterprise	28.4	22.0	31.6	32.8	22.2	25.3	27.7
Regular wage/salaried	7.2	5.7	6.8	11.0	6.4	10.9	7.4
Causal in public work	0.2	0.2	0.1	0.2	0.2	0.1	0.2
Causal in other work	33.9	49.4	29.1	16.7	30.8	28.8	33.3
Total	100	100	100	100	100	100	100

Source: Table 5.4, Sachar Committee Report.

The Table 3.5 figures show that in urban areas most of the Muslim males and females were engaged either as own account worker in household enterprises or regular wage or salaried workers or unpaid family workers in household enterprises or as casual labourers in other works. If we analyze the engagement of Muslims by sectors, industry and occupation groups, we notice that majority of the Muslim males and females in urban and rural sectors were absorbed in informal sector and proprietary male and female business. Besides, most of them conducted their business in their own dwellings or in their own enterprises and many of them were employed in employers enterprises and at construction sites. In the same way, several of them were busy in agriculture, livestock, forestry, manufacturing and wholesale and retail trade. Among occupational groups their participation was mostly as farmers, fishermen, hunters, loggers, sales agents, transport and equipment operators and production related workers. As against this, most of the other segments of the Indian society were employed in formal sectors, government and public departments, public and private limited companies as professionals, managers and technocrats.

It is worth mentioning that the economic conditions of Muslims have been affected due to several factors and one of the factors is high percentage of younger generation in the age group of 1-15 years and low participation of women in the gainful activities. The participation ratio of Muslim males and females in rural as well as urban areas as per the table 3.6 is relatively lower compared to other socio-religious groups of the country:

From the Table 3.6 statistics it is abundantly clear that overall Worker Population Ratios among Muslims was lowest at 54.9 compared to 71.4 for SCs/STs, 67.3 for Hindu OBCs and 64.5 for all minorities. Likewise, for females it was merely 25.2 as against 54.9 among SCs/STs, 48.3 in Hindu OBCs and 47.2 for all other minorities. Besides, Muslims were far behind in urban areas as well as rural areas for both sexes. The partial impact of Muslims low worker participation ratio and engagement in periphery occupations and in least paid jobs is that the poverty level among them is highest compared to

Table 3.6: Worker Population Ratios (WPR) by Socio-Religious Categories, 2004-05(Principal and Subsidiary Status, (15-64 years)

Social Group		*Urban*	*Rural*	*Male*	*Female*	*Total*
Hindus	All Hindus	53.1	70.3	84.9	46.1	65.8
	SCs/STs	56.3	74.5	87.3	54.9	71.4
	OBCs	56.4	70.5	85.8	48.3	67.3
	UC	49.0	63.5	80.8	33.1	57.4
Muslims		51.1	57.0	84.4	25.2	54.9
Other Minorities		51. 6	70.2	81.8	47.2	64.5
All		52.7	68.9	84.6	43.6	64.4

Source: Table 5.1 Sachar Committee Report.

others sections of the society. According to Tables 8.3 and 8.4(Sachar Committee Report), the poverty incidence among Muslims in urban areas during 2004-05 was to the extent of 38.4 compared to 36.4 for SCs/STs, 25.1 for Hindu OBCs, 8.3 General Hindus and 12.2 for other Minorities. In the same way, in rural areas it was at the level of 26.9 as against 34.8 for SCs/STs, 19.5 for Hindu OBCs, 9.0 for General Hindus and 14.3 for other Minorities. Moreover, the poverty incidence among Muslims as per Appendix Tables 8.5 (Sachar Committee Report) between 1983 and 2004-05 in urban areas came down from 53 to 44 compared to 55 to 46 for SCs/STs, 32 to 22 for other Hindus, 36 to 27 for all Hindus and 27 to 16 for all others. In rural areas the poverty incidence came down among Muslims from 43 to 33 as against 54 to 41 among SCs/STs, 33 to 21 for other Hindus, 40 to 28 for all Hindus and from 25 to 18 for all others. It means that not only Muslims were far behind Hindus, other Minorities and even SCs/STs in matters of poverty incidences but the rate of fall of poverty incidence among them too was lower compared to other segments of the society. The impact of poverty is reflected in the low Mean Per Capita Expenditure (MPCE) of Muslims. As per Table Appendix 8.2 (Sachar Committee Report) the MPCE for Muslims in urban areas during 2004-05 at current prices was Rs. 804 compared to Rs.793 for SCs/STs, Rs. 1008 for Hindu OBCs and Rs. 1385 for General Hindus. Likewise, in rural areas as per Appendix Table 8.3 (Sachar Committee Report) the MPCE for Muslims was Rs. 501 as against Rs. 534 for SCs/STs, Rs. 652 for Hindu OBCs, and Rs. 705 for Hindu General. As a matter of fact the relative deprivation in terms of consumption expenditure among Muslims in urban areas is much higher for most of the people are either petty shopkeepers or artisans and labourers. Actually the largest proportion of Muslims fall in the range of Rs. 400-Rs. 500 and about half of them are in the expenditure range of Rs. 300-Rs 600. Besides, the condition of Muslims in relative terms is miserable in towns with less than 50,000 people and between 50,000 and 2 lakh population. If we look at the different levels of income as per the Table 3.7, we find that Muslims are comparatively weaker at the lower, middle and higher levels of income:

Table 3.7: Distribution of different levels of income in various Socio-Religious Categories

SRC	*Urban*			*Rural*			*Total*		
	Low Income	*Middle Income*	*High Income*	*Low Income*	*Middle Income*	*High Income*	*Low Income*	*Middle Income*	*High Income*
H. Gen	8.3	58.4	33.3	9.3	84.1	6.6	8.9	73.9	17.2
H.SCs/STs	44.8	32.2	23.1	25.6	71.3	3.1	28.6	65.1	6.3
H-OBCs	21.1	74.6	4.3	27.2	72.1	0.7	25.9	72.6	1.5
Muslims	38.6	53.1	8.3	26.9	70.8	2.2	30.8	65.0	4.2
All others	11.8	53.7	34.5	13.8	74.7	11.5	13.2	68.6	18.2
Total	22.9	57.7	19.4	22.9	73.9	3.2	22.9	69.8	7.3

Source: Appendix Table 10.4, Sachar Committee Report,

Table 3.8: Share of Muslims recruited through State Public Services Commissions during the last 5 years. (Recommended/Selected for recruitment: 63,402)

Category	*All*	*Hindus*				*Muslims*	*Other Minorities*
		All Hindus	*SCs/STs*	*OBCs*	*Upper Castes*		
Higher Positions	25.4	88.8	20.9	22.7	45.3	3.2(20.7)	8.0
Lower Positions	74.6	98.0	35.2	29.0	33.9	1.6(10.4)	0.3
Group 'A'	3.6	82.2	10.3	23.7	39.2	7.5(48.6)	10.3
Group 'B'	12.4	86.4	19.8	21.2	45.3	2.2(14.3)	11.5
Group 'C'	21.1	95.8	12.6	20.8	62.4	3.0(19.4)	12
Group 'D'	53.4	98.9	44.1	32.2	22.6	1.1(7.1)	0.0

Source: Table 9.7, Sachar Committee Report.

From the Table 3.7 it is evident that in low income group in urban areas there were 44.8% Hindu SCs/STs and 38.6% Muslims compared to merely 8.3% General Hindus, 21.1% Hindu OBCs and 11.8% all others. Likewise, in Middle and High income group the number of General Hindus, Hindu OBCs and all others was greater compared to Hindu SCs/STs and Muslims. Similarly, in matters of low income in rural areas Muslims, Hindu OBCs and Hindu SCs/STs were in greater numbers compared to Hindu General and others. In the same way, in matters of Middle income all segments exceeded Muslims including Hindu SCs/STs and Hindu OBCs. Moreover, save Hindu OBCs all other sections of the society including the SCs/STs were better situated compared to Muslims in rural areas. If we look at the overall picture, we observe that major portion of Muslims was in lower income group compared to the rest including SCs/STs and Hindu OBCs. As against this, Hindu General, Hindu SCs/STs, Hindu OBCs and all others were in greater number in matters of Middle income compared to Muslims. However, in matters of high income Muslims were marginally better compared to SCs/STs and Hindu OBCs.

Painful Scenario in Government Sector at Macro Level

The most disturbing aspect is that the proportion of Muslims in government jobs is very low which has created in them a sense of alienation and dejection. The glimpse of the employment position in Government sector can be seen from Table 3.8 showing the share of Muslims recruited through State Public Services Commissions during the last five years.

Figures in parenthesis in Table 3.8 are ratios of Muslim share in their population share in per cent terms.

The Table 3.8 reveals that out of Higher positions, 88.8% were captured by the Hindus and the share of Muslims was merely 3.2%. Even the other Minorities which are nearly 25% of Muslims succeeded in getting 8.0% share. Interestingly the share of Hindu SCs/STs was 20.9% and that of Hindu OBCs to the extent of 22.7% and the Upper Castes captured 45.3% which was much larger than their population share. Similarly, among the lower positions the share of Muslims was merely 1.6% compared to 35.2% for SCs/STs, 29.0% Hindu OBCs and

Table 3.9. Share of Employment in Indian Railways according to SRCs (Total No. 14,18,747)

Category	*All*	*Hindus*			*Muslims*	*Other Minorities*
		All Hindus	*SCs/STs*	*Other Hindus*		
Higher Positions	1.3	92.8	18.2	74.6	3.0(22.4)	4.3
Lower Positions	98.7	88.6	22.5	66.1	5.0(37.3)	6.4
Group 'A'	0.7	93.8	17.8	76.0	2.5(18.7)	3.7
Group 'B'	0.6	91.5	19.0	72.6	3.4(25.4)	5.0
Group 'C'	59.7	88.5	22.0	66.5	4.9(36.6)	6.5
Group 'D'	37.4	88.7	23.4	65.3	5.0(37.3)	6.3

Source: Appendix Table 9.1, Sachar Committee Report.

Table 3.10: Share of Employment in National Security Agencies (No. of Employees 5,19,008)

Category	*All*	*Hindus*			*Muslims*	*Other Minorities*
		All Hindus	*SCs/STs*	*Other Hindus*		
Higher Positions	3.9	87.5	11.7	75.8	3.6(26.9)	8.9
Lower Positions	96.1	88.7	24.4	64.4	4.6(34.3)	6.7
Group 'A'	1.3	86.0	11.9	74.1	3.1(23.1)	10.9
Group 'B'	2.6	88.2	11.6	76.6	3.9(29.1)	7.9
Group 'C'	91.5	88.7	23.8	64.9	4.6(34.3)	6.7
Group 'D'	4.2	89.3	36.8	52.5	4.3(32.1)	6.4
Others	0.4	85.3	24.2	61.1	3.3(24.6)	11.3

Source: Appendix Table 9.2, Sachar Committee Report.

33.9% Hindu Upper Castes. Virtually 98.0% lower posts were retained by the Hindus. Likewise, in Groups 'A', 'B' and 'C' too Muslims share was negligible and most of these posts were shared by the Hindu SCs/STs, OBCs and Upper Castes. The misfortune of Muslims is that their share in Group 'D' posts which normally do not require special qualifications was merely 1.1% compared to 44.1% for Hindu SCs/STs and 32.2% for Hindu OBCs and 22.6% Hindu Upper Castes.

If we analyze the situation of government jobs sector wise we observe more or less the same situation. Table 3.9 reveals the share of Muslims in Indian Railways which is supposed to be receptive to Muslims:

Figures within parenthesis in Table 3.9 are ratios of Muslims share to their population.

The table 3.9 shows that Muslims' share among Higher and lower positions as well as in Groups 'A', 'B', 'C', and 'D' was lower than that of SCs/STs, other Hindus, all Hindus and other Minorities. Their deficit is amply visible among all the segments and it appears as if they are a non entity. In no sector they could touch the double digit. They could not go beyond 5.0% even in Group 'D' posts which require no specialized qualifications and training. Other Minorities which are one fourth of Muslims exceeded in all categories compared to the Muslims and the SCs/STs too were far ahead of Muslims in every segment.

The employment situation with regards to Muslims in National Security Agencies too was dismal which is exhibited by the Table 3.10.

Figures within parenthesis Table 3.10 are ratios of Muslims share to their population.

Regrettably, the Table 3.10 repeats the same story as was found in matters of employment in Indian Railways. Here the picture is worse than what we observed in case of Railways. Muslims' share in all segments of National Security agencies was much lower compared to All Hindus, SCs/STs, other Hindus and other Minorities. What to talk of all Hindus or other Hindus since they had captured most of the posts in all areas, even the situation of the SCs/STs and other Minorities too was far better compared to Muslims. In no segment

Muslims could cross 5% mark. In groups 'C' and 'D' where they could show their strength, their share was 4.6% and 4.3% respectively. These figures frighten Muslims and compel them to think that there is little space left for them in the government sector. Since the figures pertaining to Hindu OBCs, Muslim OBCs and Muslim General were not provided in the above table, we have compared the employment position of Muslim OBCs, Muslim general and the Hindu OBCs in various Government sectors in the Table 3.11.

Table 3.11: Representation in Public Sector Employment

Categories	*Hindu-OBCs*	*Muslim-Gen*	*Muslim-OBCs*
Central Security Agencies			
Higher Positions	4.6	0.4	3.2
Lower positions	11.7	1.0	3.6
Grade 'A'	5.4	0.3	2.8
Group 'B'	4.1	0.5	3.4
Group 'C'	11.8	1.0	3.6
Group 'D'	10.0	1.1	3.2.
Others	1.8	0.3	3.0
Total	11.4	1.0	3.6
Railways			
Higher Positions	2.8	2.8	0.2
Lower Positions	9.4	4.5	0.4
Grade 'A'	3.5	2.3	0.2
Grade 'B'	2.0	3.3	0.1
Grade 'C'	8.7	4.6	0.3
Grade 'D'	10.5	4.5	0.5
Total	9.3	4.5	0.4
Public Sector Undertakings: Central			
Managerial-I	5.3	1.9	0.3
Managerial-II	10.4	2.6	0.2
Workers	9.2	3.1	0.8
Total	8.3	2.7	0.6

contd...

Categories	*Hindu-OBCs*	*Muslim-Gen*	*Muslim-OBCs*
State Public Services Commission: Recommended/Selected			
Higher Positions	21.0	1.9	1.2
Lower positions	29.1	0.6	0.8
Grade 'A'	18.8	6.1	1.3
Grade 'B'	20.0	0.6	1.4
Grade 'C'	19.6	1.4	0.9
Grade 'D'	32.2	0.3	0.8
Total	27.0	0.9	0.9

.*Source:* Appendix Table 10.3, Sachar Committee Report.

From the Table 3.11 figures it is abundantly clear that Muslim General and Muslim OBCs were far behind Hindu OBCs in all the segments of Public Sector employment. In Central Security Agencies the representation of Hindu OBCs in Higher Positions, Lower Positions and Grades A, B, C and D was 11.4% compared to 1.0% for Muslim General and 3.6 Muslim OBCs. Likewise, in Railways on an average Hindu OBCs in all positions and grades were to the extent of 9.3% as against 4.5% Muslim General and 0.4% Muslim OBCs. Similarly, in Central Public Sector Undertakings the participation of Hindu OBCs in Managerial-I and Managerial-II as well as workers was to the tune of 8.3% in contrast to 2.7% for Muslim General and 0.6% Muslim OBCs. In the same way, on an average the State Public Services Commission recommended and selected 27.0% OBCs in comparison to 0.9% Muslim General and 0.9% Muslim OBCs. Muslims despite constituting nearly 15% of the total population of the country could not get more than 4.6% in Central Security Agencies, 4.9% in Railways and 1.8 in various positions and grades through State Public Services Commission. These statistics behind the lines speak volumes about the miserable fate of Muslims who once upon a time were a dominant part of the Indian society.

If we look at the comprehensive picture concerning Muslim employees in Government Sector Employment the following picture emerges from Table 3.12.

Table 3.12: Muslim Employees in Government Sector Employment

Departments / Institutions Reporting	*Reported Number of Employees*	*Reported Number of Muslims Employees*	*Muslim as Percentage to reported Employees*
State Level-Departments	4452851	278385	6.3
Railways	1418747	64066	4.5
Banks and RBI	680833	15030	2.2
Security Agencies	1879134	60517	3.2
Postal Services	275841	13759	5.0
Universities	137263	6416	4.7
Employment (Excludes PSUs)	884 44 669	438 173	4.9
Central PSU's	887512	22387	3.3
State PSUs	745271	80661	10.8
All PSUs	143278	103048	7.2

Source: Table 9.1, Sachar Committee Report.

It is most unfortunate that the India's biggest minority constituting a significant part of the total population of the country has remained loser over a period of sixty years. Their share in almost all the segments of the country has been captured by other castes and classes of the society. Presently, they are conspicuous by absence in the Government sector. Their meagre presence at State Level Departments to the extent of 6.3%, in Railways to the level of 4.5% , in Banks and RBI within the range of 2.2%, in Security Agencies merely to the tune of 3.2%, in Postal Services within the magnitude of

5.0%, in Universities in the reach of 4.7%, in Central PSUs within the limit of 3.3% and in all Public Sector Utilities to the extent of 7.2% does not give them the impression that they are the significant part of the governing structure.

Muslims are also lacking in physical and social infrastructure. They are at a disadvantage vis-à-vis other sections of the society in almost all the segments of health care and welfare. Their quality of life is poor. The dearth of good Government Schools has led to high dropout rates among Muslim children. They lack health facilities and drinking water and sanitation have caused diseases, malnutrition and reduced productivity and resulted in low life expectancy. Similarly, the deficiency in the transport, communication and credit facilities has affected social and economic status of Muslim households. It has been generally observed that most of the infrastructural facilities are inversely related to the Muslim population. As the number of Muslims increases in any village, these facilities begin to decline and vice versa. For instance, while 82% of small villages with less than 10% Muslims had educational facilities but this proportion decreased to 69% with substantial Muslim population. Likewise, there was scarcity of medical facilities in large villages with larger Muslim population and nearly 40% villages with considerable number of Muslims did not have any medical facility. In the same way, the availability of drinking water, electricity, modern fuel, bus stop, Post Offices and all-weather roads among Muslim concentrated areas were lower compared to other segments of the society. Besides, fearing for the security, Muslims have increasingly resorted to ghettoisation which has made them the easy prey of the neglect of Municipal Corporation and other government agencies. Muslims also complain of the step-brotherly treatment to Urdu. They emphasize that their children are not provided education in their mother tongue despite the three-language formula and the Urdu Schools are ill-equipped in matters of teachers, quality of books and infrastructural and financial facilities. Their all the grievances and perceptions may not be true but the fact is that they are at a disadvantage in these areas and these deficiencies are affecting the growth and development of Muslim Community. Besides, the facts and figures that we have provided above in the light of the growth profile of OBC and SCs/STs amply prove that they have certainly lagged behind in the social, economic, educational and political fields compared to even the downtrodden sections of Indian society. Without going into the causes or fault finding it is in the national interest as well as in the interest of Muslims that they too should be treated as a depressed, marginalized and backward section of the society as a whole and they too should be provided the same incentives which were provided to up lift the Scheduled Castes and the Scheduled Tribes and Backward Classes. Without this it is next to impossible for them to come out of the rut.

Muslim Identity Reflected from their Depleting Parameters

Muslims in India have actually become a distinct identity due to their depleted social and cultural frame of reference, weak educational background and poor economic conditions. One can easily spot them by their unique dress code, conservative pattern of life and Urdu ascent. Besides, they are more urbanized than Hindus and Sikhs, their sex ratio at 936 is above the normal average, their 41.0% females marry at the age between 10-17 years which is highest compared to all and the proportion of Muslims elderly is lowest at 5.75%. Likewise, their average size of households at 3.50 is highest among the country. They have literacy level lower than the national average and compared to all religions Muslims are lowest at Middle, Secondary, Senior Secondary, Diploma and Graduation level. Their percentage declines from 65.31 at Primary level to 15.14 at Middle, 10.98 at Secondary, 4.53 at Senior Secondary, 0.41 at Diploma and 3.6 at Graduation Level. Similarly, Muslims are lagging in Immunization Programme and healthcare indicators. The use of contraceptives is least among them and the average number of children to the extent of 5.72 born to married women 40-49 years is highest among Muslims. In the same way, only 23.76% Muslims share Pacca Houses which is lowest and the percentage of households living in Kaccha Houses is highest at 34.63%. Moreover, the ratio of those living in rented houses is highest among Muslims at 43.74% and the proportion using electricity in urban areas is lowest at 78.78%. Over and above this, the lowest work participation rate at 31.3% at the national level is found only among Muslims. Besides, only 20% Muslims are cultivators, the proportion of self-employed workers among Muslim females to the tune of 75% is higher than any other religious community involved in household industry work. Furthermore, among the States of Maharashtra, Punjab, Tamil Nadu, Uttar Pradesh and West Bengal Muslims have lowest average monthly income at Rs.1832. Compared to all, Muslims have the highest young persons dependency ratio at 778 and the lowest dependency ratio at 109 among the old. These factors certainly reveal their miserable lot. They are far behind other religious segments in the areas of industry, trade and commerce, entrepreneurship, and governing sector. Most of them have frustration lit large on their foreheads, despondency visible from their piercing eyes and depression reflecting from their conversations. In Muslim concentration areas, there is no out let for their products, they seldom get loans from the banks and the Wakfs too do not help in solving their problems. They lack professional degrees and diplomas as well as technical and vocational training. The most backward sections of Muslims such as faqueers, gorkuns and halalkhores and those who lost their trade due to modernization of industries live in critical conditions due to lack of demand of their professions. Similarly, the artisans like weavers, spinners, oil crushers etc. are languishing due to their old techniques. The incidence of poverty among Muslims is highest in urban areas and about one-third Muslims live in wretched conditions without basic facilities like drinking water, toilet and electricity facilities. There is a dearth of modern educational facilities in Muslim localities as a consequence of which they fail to enter into the educational mainstream. All these factors and many more amply reveal that Muslims are on the lowest pedestal of the society and they need affirmative actions to bring them within the national milieu failing which they would fit in the vacuum created by the upward development of the Backward Classes and Scheduled Castes permanently.

4

The Depressing Profile of Muslims in Various States of India

So far we have studied about the depressing condition of Muslims at all India level. Now we shall reflect on their miserable conditions at the levels of various states to show that they are in an urgent need of quick and special treatment. Factually Muslims are a largest minority and no country can afford that such a large minority remains backward for ever. All civilized societies are committed to uphold the equality of citizens and all governments of the world are obliged to preserve, protect and assure the rights of minorities in matters of religion, culture and language. The United Nations Declaration on the rights of ethnic, religious and linguistic minorities also emphasizes on the promotion and protection of the rights of numerically marginalized sections of the society. Indian Constitution ensures equality before law and prohibits discrimination on the grounds of religion, race, caste, sex and place of birth. It ensures freedom of conscience and the right to freely profess, practice and propagate religion as well as guarantees the right to manage religious institutions, religious affairs and also protects minorities rights to conserve their language, script and culture. Besides the Constitutional provisions, there are number of other directives that safeguard the interests of minorities in the country. All enlightened cultures are very particular about the rights of the minorities and all the meaningful governments go beyond their prescribed powers to help and assist the minorities. As a matter of fact the compassionate and impartial manner in which any state in the world behaves towards its minorities is a real test of its being a just, equitable and welfare state.

Presently a significant public debate on the educational, social, political, cultural and economic conditions of Muslims is going on in the country especially after Sachar Committee Report and Ranganath Misra Commission findings. Most of the findings reveal that Muslims have lagged behind in the process of development. There is a vast development gap together with the feeling of extreme neglect which has disheartened the largest minority of the country. Apart from facing the perceived identity and security crisis, Muslims are facing several issues concerning equity, equality and justice. The perception of deprivation and inequity is practically widespread in every field among Muslims especially due to discrimination that they face due to differences in identity. The irony of fate is that despite suffering adversely in almost all the indicators of growth, there is a charge of appeasement against them as a consequence of which only a few political parties are willing to provide them some space in the national reconstruction. The ghost of separate electorate which caused Partition is perhaps looming so large on the political horizon of the country that practically every political party is afraid of conceding reservations to Muslims despite their well proven and well authenticated economic decadence. The author would try to bring before the government, civil society and the majority and minority segments of the country the adversely depressing socio-economic conditions of Indian Muslims at states level to convince the masses that Muslims are in a poor shape both at the micro as well as macro levels and need affirmative actions to save them from falling in the debris.

A Brief Discouraging Profile of Muslims

In the previous chapter we have tried to provide a macro view of Muslims' decadence. In this chapter we would like to show their deplorable conditions at micro levels in various states of the country. If we look in the light of facts and figures provided by Sachar Committee Report at the profile of various growth signs in various states of the country, we find that Muslims lack in most of them at all India as well as all

States level. According to the figures of 2004-05 General Muslims were 59.3% and the Muslim OBCs were 40.7% of the total Muslim population as compared to 31.1% Hindu SCs/ STs, 43.0% Hindu OBCs and 25.9% Hindu General but for all practical purposes there is no difference between general Muslims and Muslim OBCs in matters of socio-economic conditions. Greater number of Muslim OBCs lived in Kerala, Uttar Pradesh, Bihar, Jharkhand, Karnataka, Uttaranchal, Rajasthan, Haryana, Tamil Nadu and Punjab. As against this, the percentage of General Muslims was larger in West Bengal, Assam, Jammu & Kashmir, Delhi, Maharashtra, Andhra Pradesh, Gujarat, Madhya Pradesh, Orissa and Himachal Pradesh. Muslims unique socio economic conditions are also reflected in the growth of their population, sex ratio, mortality and fertility rates. The population growth among Muslims at all India level between 1991 and 2001 was 29.5% compared to 21.5% among all religions. The rate of growth of Muslim population between 1991 and 2001 compared to all religions was on the higher side among all States of the country. The trend in the sex ratio reveals that during 2001 it was 936 compared to 933 among all religions. The sex ratio among Muslims during 2001 was better compared to all religions in Kerala, Uttar Pradesh, Bihar, Assam, Gujarat, Rajasthan, Tamil Nadu, Madhya Pradesh and Haryana. However, it was lower in West Bengal, Jammu & Kashmir, Karnataka, Delhi, Maharashtra, Andhra Pradesh Orissa, Punjab, Uttaranchal, Jharkhand and Chattisgarh. The relative larger increase in Muslim population can be assigned to lower child mortality rate, high fertility rate, less use of contraceptive, illiteracy and poverty among Muslims. The Infant Mortality Rate (IMR) among Muslims during 1998-99 was 59 compared to 73 for all, 77 for Hindus. Similarly, the Under 5 Mortality Rate among Muslims too was 83 in contrast to101 for all and 107 for Hindus. The Infant Mortality Rate and the Under 5 Mortality Rate was higher among Muslims in practically all the States of the country such as West Bengal, Kerala, Uttar Pradesh, Bihar, Assam, Jammu & Kashmir, Karnataka, Maharashtra, Andhra Pradesh, Gujarat, Rajasthan, Madhya Pradesh, Haryana and Tamil Nadu. Similarly, the Total Fertility Rate and Cumulative fertility rate among Muslims during 1998-99 was 3.6 and 5.7 compared to 2.9 and 4.5 among all religions and 2.8 and 4.3

among Hindus respectively. These rates were high in contrast to all religions among all states of India including West Bengal, Kerala, Uttar Pradesh, Bihar, Assam, Jammu & Kashmir, Karnataka, Maharashtra, Andhra Pradesh, Gujarat, Rajasthan and Tamil Nadu. Only 37% Muslims used contraceptives during 1998-99 in comparison to 49% Hindus, 52% Christians, 65% Sikhs, 65 Buddhists and 48% all. The contraceptive prevalence rate among Muslims during 1998-99 was on the lower side compared to Hindus, others and all in Andhra Pradesh, Assam, Bihar, Jharkhand, Gujarat, Haryana, Jammu & Kashmir, Karnataka, Kerala, Madhya Pradesh, Chhattisgarh, Maharashtra, Punjab, Rajasthan, Tamil Nadu, Uttar Pradesh, Uttaranchal and West Bengal. Another special feature of Muslim population in the country is that the trend of urbanization among them is on the higher side compared to all because they are situated unfavorably at rural level and hence they have to migrate to the cities to earn the livelihood. During 2001 the urbanization trend among Muslims was to the extent of 35.7% compared to 27.8% among all religions. Save West Bengal, Kerala, Assam, Jammu & Kashmir, Punjab and Haryana it was on the higher sides in Uttar Pradesh, Bihar, Karnataka, Delhi, Maharashtra, Andhra Pradesh, Gujarat, Rajasthan, Madhya Pradesh, Tamil Nadu, Orissa and Madhya Pradesh.

The Disheartening Literacy Rate at the Level of States

If we analyze literacy rate among various states during 2001, we find that the literacy level among Muslims at all states level was highly discouraging. Table 4.1 quoted by Sachar Committee shows the dismal picture of State-wise literacy levels:

Table 4.1: State-wise Literacy Levels-2001

State (Muslim Population%)	*Total*				
	All	*Hindus*	*SCs/STs*	*Muslims*	*All Others*
India (13.4)	64.8	65.1	52.2	59.1	70.8
West Bengal (25.2)	68.6	72.4	56.1	57.5	81.6
Kerala (24.7)	90.9	90.2	80.8	89.4	93.1

contd...

State	*Total*				
	All	*Hindus*	*SCs / STs*	*Muslims*	*All Others*
Uttar Pradesh (18.5)	56.3	58.0	46.2	47.8	62.2
Bihar (16.5)	47.0	47.9	28.5	42.0	52.6
Assam (30.9)	63.3	70.0	64.0	48.4	71.3
Jammu & Kashmir (67.0) 55.5	71.2	46.5	47.3	100.0	
Jharkhand (13.8)	53.6	54.6	39.7	55.6	63.7
Karnataka (12.2)	66.6	65.6	51.5	70.1	71.1
Uttaranchal (11.9)	71.6	74.1	63.4	51.1	77.4
Delhi (11.7)	81.7	82.8	70.8	66.6	86.5
Maharashtra (10.6)	76.9	76.2	64.3	78.1	80.0
Andhra Pradesh (9.2)	60.5	59.4	48.9	68.0	63.3
Gujarat (9.1)	69.1	68.3	55.3	73.5	72.8
Rajasthan (8.5)	60.4	60.2	49.1	56.6	66.1
Madhya Pradesh (6.4)	63.7	62.8	48.7	70.3	71.7
Haryana (5.8)	67.9	69.4	55.4	40.0	72.9
Tamil Nadu (5.6)	73.5	72.0	62.1	82.9	75.8
Orissa (2.1)	63.1	63.3	45.2	71.3	74.0
Himachal Pradesh (2.0)	76.5	76.8	69.6	57.5	79.8
Chhattisgarh (2.0)	64.7	63.9	55.3	82.5	71.3
Punjab (1.6)	69.7	74.6	56.2	51.2	75.4

Figures within parenthesis are % share of the Muslim population
Source: Appendix Table 4.1, Sachar Committee Report.

The Table 4.1 reveals that the literacy rate among Muslims was to the tune of 59.1% compared to 65.1% for Hindus, 52.2% for SCs/STs and 70.8% for all others. In West Bengal which had 25.2% Muslim population during 2001, the literacy rate was 68.6% compared to 72.4% in Hindus, 81.6% in all others, 56.1% in SCs/STs and 68.6% in All. Likewise, in Kerala constituting 24.7% of the total population, it was 89.4% among Muslims as against 90.2% for Hindus, 93.1% for all others and 80.8% for SCs/STs. The literacy situation among Muslims in Uttar Pradesh too was not satisfactory. Literacy rate among Muslims was 47.8% compared to 58.0% for Hindus, 62.2% for all others and 46.2% for SCs/STs. In Bihar Muslims forming 18.5% of the total population the literacy rate was 42.0% in contrast to 47.9% for Hindus, 52.6% for all others and 28.5% for SCs/STs. In Assam Muslims constituted 30.9% of the total population, but literacy was merely 48.4% in contrast to70.0% Hindus, 71.3% for all others and 64.0 for SCs/STs. In Jammu and Kashmir despite being a majority Muslim state constituting 67.0% Muslim population, the literacy rate among Muslims was 47.3% compared to 71.2% for Hindus, 100 for all others and 46.5% for SCs/STs. The condition in Jharkhand was slightly better for Muslims constituting 13.8% of the total population but literacy rate among them was 55.6% compared to 54.6% for Hindus, 63.7% for all others and 39.7% for SCs/STs. In Karnataka with 12.2% Muslim population, the literacy rate among Muslims was better. It stood at 70.1% as against 65.6% for Hindus, 71.1% for all others and 51.5% for SCs/STS. In Uttaranchal with11.9% Muslim population, the literacy rate was 51.1% in contrast to 74.1% for Hindus, 77.4% for all others and 63.4% for SCs/STs. In Delhi, Muslims with 11.7% of the total population, had literacy rate at 66.6% in contrast to 82.8% for Hindus, 86.5% for all others and 70.8% for SCs/STs. In Maharashtra with 10.6% Muslim population, the literacy rate among Muslims was 78.1% compared to 76.2% for Hindus, 80.0% for all others and 64.3% for SCs/STs. Similarly, in Andhra Pradesh with 9.2% Muslim population, it was 68.0% compared to 59.4% for Hindus, 63.3% for all others and 48.9% for SCs/STs. In Gujarat with 9.1% Muslim population, the literacy rate among Muslims was better at 73.5% compared to 68.3% for Hindus, 72.8% for all others and 55.3% for SCs/STs. While in Rajasthan with 8.5% Muslim population the literacy

Table 4.2. State-wise Literacy Levels Gender (Urban) 2001

	Urban All					*Urban Male*					*Urban Females*				
State	*A*	*H*	*SC/ ST*	*M*	*O*	*A*	*H*	*SC/ ST*	*M*	*O*	*A*	*H*	*SC/ ST*	*M*	*O*
India (13.4)	80	81	68	70	85	86	88	78	76	90	73	74	58	63	78
West Bengal (25.2)	81	84	68	66	87	86	89	77	72	91	76	78	59	59	82
Kerala (24.7)	93	93	87	91	95	96	96	92	95	97	91	91	83	87	93
Uttar Pradesh (18.5)	70	76	58	55	81	77	83	69	61	87	62	68	45	47	73
Bihar (16.5)	72	74	50	64	77	80	82	61	71	85	63	64	37	57	68
Assam (30.9)	85	87	80	72	89	90	92	87	78	93	80	83	73	66	84
Jammu & Kashmir (67)	72	85	68	63	88	80	91	77	72	93	62	77	58	52	81
Jharkhand (13.8)	79	79	63	78	84	87	88	74	84	91	70	70	50	71	76
Karnataka (12.2)	81	81	68	76	85	87	88	78	80	91	74	74	59	71	79
Uttaranchal (11.9)	81	86	73	59	88	87	91	82	67	93	75	79	62	51	83
Delhi (11.7)	82	83	71	67	87	87	89	81	72	91	75	76	59	59	81
Maharashtra (10.6)	85	86	77	80	88	91	92	87	85	93	79	80	68	75	82
Andhra Pradesh(9.2)	76	76	67	73	78	83	84	76	79	86	69	69	58	67	71

Table 4.2 (Contd.)

	Urban All					*Urban Male*					*Urban Females*				
State	*A*	*H*	*SC/ ST*	*M*	*O*	*A*	*H*	*SC/ ST*	*M*	*O*	*A*	*H*	*SC/ ST*	*M*	*O*
Gujarat (9.1)	82	82	73	76	84	88	89	83	84	90	75	75	63	68	77
Rajasthan (8.5)	76	78	61	64	83	86	88	77	76	92	65	66	44	50	74
Madhya Pradesh (6.4)	79	80	65	74	85	87	88	77	81	92	70	70	52	68	77
Haryana (5.8)	79	80	60	53	83	86	86	71	63	89	71	72	48	40	76
Tamil Nadu (5.6)	83	82	71	84	84	89	88	80	90	90	76	75	62	78	78
Orissa (2.1)	81	81	63	74	86	88	88	75	81	92	73	73	50	66	80
Himachal Pradesh (2.0)	89	90	82	73	91	92	93	88	73	94	85	85	74	72	88
Chhattisgarh (2.1)	81	79	70	86	83	89	89	82	92	91	71	69	58	80	74
Punjab (1.6)	79	80	62	55	84	83	83	69	60	87	74	75	54	48	80

Figures within parenthesis are% share of Muslim population

Source: Appendix Table 4.1a, Sachar Committee Report.

rate among Muslims was 56.6% in contrast to 60.2% for Hindus, 66.1% for all others and 49.1% for SCs/STs. Madhya Pradesh with 6.4% Muslim population had higher literacy rate among Muslims to the tune of 70.3% compared to 62.8% for Hindus, 71.7% for all others and 48.7% for SCs/STs. Haryana with 5.8% Muslim population had literacy rate among Muslims to the extent of 40.0% compared to 69.4% for Hindus, 72.9% for all others and 55.4% for SCs/STs. Tamil Nadu with merely5.6% Muslim population had better literary rate at 82.9% compared to 72.0% for Hindus, 75.8% for all others and 62.1% for SCs/STs .Orissa with 2.1% Muslim population too had better literacy rate among Muslims at 71.3% compared to 63.3% for Hindus, 74.0% for all others and 45.2% for SCs/STs. Himachal Pradesh with 2.0% Muslim population had 57.5% literacy rate contrasted to 76.8% for Hindus, 79.8% for all others and 69.6% for SCs/STs. In Chhattisgarh Muslims with merely 2.0% population had better literacy rate at 82.5% compared to 63.9% for Hindus, 71.3% for all others and 55.3% for SCs/STs. Lastly, Punjab with 1.6% Muslim population had 51.2% literacy rate as against 74.6% for Hindus, 75.4% for all others and 56.2% for SCs/STs Thus, we find that in matters of literacy rate Muslims are generally far below Hindus and all others in most of the states of India. Except in West Bengal, Kerala, Uttar Pradesh, Jammu & Kashmir and Rajasthan where they are more or less equal to SCs/STs, they are marginally better off compared SCs/STs in Bihar, Jharkhand, Karnataka, Andhra Pradesh, Gujarat, Madhya Pradesh Tamil Nadu, Orissa and Chhattisgarh. However, they are far below SCs/STs in Uttaranchal, Delhi, Haryana, Himachal Pradesh and Punjab.

The state-wise literacy level by gender in urban areas during 2001 was highly unfavorable for Muslims. The following Table cited by Sachar Committee Report shows the State-wise Literacy Levels by Gender in urban areas during 2001.

Table 4.2 figures exhibit that in urban areas Muslims including males and females taken together lagged behind in literacy rate compared to Hindus as well as all others. The literacy level among Muslims males and females was to the extent of 70 compared to 80 for all, 81 for Hindus, 68 for SCs/STs and 85 for all others. They were worse off compared to SCs/STs in West Bengal, Uttar Pradesh, Assam, Jammu &

Table 4.3 State-wise Literacy levels by Gender (Rural)-2001

State	*Rural All*					*Rural Male*					*Rural Female*				
	A	*H*	*SC/ST*	*M*	*O*	*A*	*H*	*SC/ST*	*M*	*O*	*A*	*H*	*SC/ST*	*M*	*O*
India (13.4)	59	59	49	53	64	71	72	61	62	77	46	46	36	43	52
West Bengal (25.2)	63	67	54	56	78	73	77	67	63	86	53	56	41	48	68
Kerala ((24.7)	90	89	80	89	93	94	93	85	93	95	87	85	74	85	90
Uttar Pradesh (18.5)	53	54	44	44	58	67	69	59	55	72	37	38	28	32	41
Bihar (16.5)	44	45	27	39	49	57	59	39	49	64	30	30	14	28	34
Assam (30.9)	60	66	62	47	67	68	75	72	54	76	51	57	52	38	58
Jammu& Kashmir (67)	50	65	57	43	69	62	77	68	54	80	37	52	45	30	55
Jharkhand (13.8)	46	46	37	4754	61	62	50	61	71	30	29	23	3336		
Karnataka (12.2)	59	59	47	62	64	70	70	58	72	75	48	47	35	52	53

Table 4.3 (contd..)

State	*Rural All*					*Rural Male*					*Rural Female*				
	A	*H*	*SC/ST*	*M*	*O*	*A*	*H*	*SC/ST*	*M*	*O*	*A*	*H*	*SC/ST*	*M*	*O*
Uttaranchal (11.9)	68	70	62	46	73	82	85	76	56	88	55	57	46	34	60
Delhi (11.7)	78	79	71	61	81	87	88	82	70	89	67	68	57	49	72
Maharashtra (10.6)	70	70	59	73	74	82	82	72	83	85	58	58	47	62	62
Andhra Pradesh (9.2)	55	54	46	61	57	65	65	56	73	68	44	43	35	48	46
Gujarat (9.1)	61	61	51	69	65	74	74	63	81	78	48	47	39	57	51
Rajasthan (8.5)	55	55	47	50	60	72	72	64	67	77	37	37	28	31	43
Madhya Pradesh (6.4)	58	57	46	64	66	72	71	59	77	80	43	42	32	49	50
Gujarat (9.1)	61	61	51	69	65	74	74	63	81	78	48	47	39	57	51
Rajasthan (8.5)	55	55	47	50	60	72	72	64	67	77	37	37	28	31	43

Table 4.3 (contd..)

State	*Rural All*					*Rural Male*					*Rural Female*				
	A	*H*	*SC/ST*	*M*	*O*	*A*	*H*	*SC/ST*	*M*	*O*	*A*	*H*	*SC/ST*	*M*	*O*
Madhya Pradesh (6.4)	58	57	46	64	66	72	71	59	77	80	43	42	32	49	50
Haryana (5.8)	63	65	54	38	68	75	77	66	55	80	49	51	41	19	54
Tamil Nadu (5.6)	66	65	58	79	68	77	76	69	88	80	55	54	48	72	57
Orissa (2.1)	60	60	44	69	71	73	73	58	79	83	47	47	29	60	59
Himachal Pradesh (2.0)	75	75	69	55	78	85	85	79	65	87	66	66	58	43	69
Chattisgarh (2.0)	60	60	54	76	67	74	74	67	87	80	47	47	40	64	53
Punjab (1.6)	65	68	54	48	70	71	76	62	54	76	58	60	46	40	64

The figures in the parenthesis are % share of the Muslim population.

Source: Appendix Table 4.1b, Sachar Committee Report.

Kashmir, Uttaranchal, Delhi, Haryana, Himachal Pradesh and Punjab. They were more or less equal to SCs/STs in Kerala, Maharashtra, Andhra Pradesh, Gujarat and Rajasthan. Similarly, the urban males of Muslims were behind all urban males of Hindus and all others. The literacy level among urban Muslim males was 76 in contrast to 86 for all, 88 for Hindus, 78 for SCs/STs and 90 for all others. They were even behind SCs/STs urban males in West Bengal, Uttar Pradesh, Assam, Jammu & Kashmir, Uttaranchal, Delhi, Haryana, Himachal Pradesh and Punjab. They were more or less equal in other states. In the same way, Muslim urban females were far behind all urban females of Hindus and all others. They stood at 63 in comparison to 73 for all, 74 for Hindus, 58 for SCs/STs and 78 for all others in matters of literacy level. They were more or less equal to urban female of SCs/STs in West Bengal, Kerala, Uttar Pradesh, Jammu & Kashmir, Delhi, Maharashtra, Andhra Pradesh, Gujarat, Rajasthan, Haryana and slightly better in Jharkhand, Madhya Pradesh, Tamil Nadu, Orissa, and Chhattisgarh. However, they were inferior to SCs/STs urban females in Assam, Uttaranchal, Haryana, Himachal Pradesh and Punjab.

Practically the same was the literacy condition of Muslim males and Muslim females in rural areas because both these segments of Muslims were far behind all India level as well as for Hindus and for all others. Table 4.3 used by Sachar Committee Report pinpoints the glaring literacy differences between Muslims and others.

The Table 4.3 figures show that rural Muslims both males and females were at the level of 53 as against 59 for all, 59 for Hindus, 49 for SCs/STs and 64 for all others. They were comparable only to SCs/STs for somewhere they were slightly better off some were slightly worse off and some where equal to them. For instance, Muslim rural males and females were slightly better in Bihar, Jharkhand, Karnataka, Maharashtra, Andhra Pradesh, Gujarat, Madhya Pradesh, Tamil Nadu, Orissa, and Chhattisgarh. They were inferior to SCs/STs rural males and females in Assam, Jammu & Kashmir, Uttaranchal, Delhi, Haryana, Himachal Pradesh and Punjab. They were, however more or less equal to SCs/STs rural males and females in West Bengal, Kerala, Uttar Pradesh and Rajasthan.

Similarly, the rural males stood at 62 with reference to 71 for all, 72 for Hindus, 61 for SCs/STs and 77 for all others. This shows that here also they were below all, Hindus and all others and slightly better off compared to SCs/STs. State-wise, the rural SCs/STs males were better than Muslim males in West Bengal, Uttar Pradesh, Assam, Jammu & Kashmir, Uttaranchal, Delhi, Haryana, Himachal Pradesh and Punjab. They were behind Muslim rural males in Kerala, Bihar, Jharkhand, Karnataka, Maharashtra, Andhra Pradesh, Tamil Naidu, Orissa and Chhattisgarh. In the same way, Muslim females were far behind all, Hindus and others as they stood at 43 in contrast to 46 for all, 46 for Hindus, 36 for SCs/STs and 52 for all. If we look at the figures at the state level we find that the SCs/STs rural females were better off in literacy rate compared to Muslim rural females in Assam, Jammu & Kashmir, Uttaranchal, Delhi, Haryana, Himachal Pradesh and Punjab and they were marginally inferior to Muslim rural females in West Bengal, Kerala, Uttar Pradesh, Bihar, Jharkhand, Karnataka, Maharashtra, Andhra Pradesh, Gujarat, Rajasthan, Madhya Pradesh, Tamil Naidu, Orissa and Chhattisgarh. Thus, we find that Muslims who were in dominant position in Uttar Pradesh, West Bengal, Assam, Bihar, Kerala, Maharashtra, Karnataka Delhi Andhra Pradesh, Madhya Pradesh, Tamil Nadu and various other states of the country have fallen behind in literacy rates in most of the states of India compared to Hindus and all others. They are comparable only to SCs/STs as compared to them they are somewhere worse off, somewhere slightly better and somewhere equal to them. Muslims of India lament that after sixty years they have been reduced to the status of SCs/STs in matters of literacy in most amongst all the states of the country.

The above facts can be further strengthened if we look at the figures of Appendix Table 4.2 (Sachar Committee report) pertaining to mean years of schooling of children aged 7-16 during 2001. We find that at All India level the average comes to 3.26 for Muslims compared to 3.95 for total, 3.35 for SCs/STs and 4.39 for all others. The mean years of schooling for Muslim Children aged 7-16 in West Bengal was 2.84 compared to 3.58 for total, 3.12 for SCs/STs and 4.51 for all others.

Likewise, the Muslims lagged behind in mean years of schooling compared to total, SCs/STs and all others in Uttar Pradesh, Assam, Uttaranchal, Delhi, Haryana, Himachal Pradesh and Punjab. They were also behind all India figure and all others in Kerala, Bihar, Jammu & Kashmir, Karnataka, Maharashtra, Gujarat and Tamil Nadu. However, they were slightly better or more or les equai to SCs/STs in Kerala, Bihar, Jammu & Kashmir, Karnataka, Maharashtra, Gujarat, Rajasthan and Tamil Nadu. Similarly, the proportion of children aged 6-14 years enrolled by SRCs during 2004-05 was 81.8 for Muslims as against 85.3 for All India, 79.7 for SCs/STs, 86.0 for Hindu OBCs, 94.9 for Hindu General and 89.9 for all others. In almost all the states the proportion of children enrolled was lower in contrast to total, Hindu OBCs, Hindu General and all others. It was lower than SCs/STs in West Bengal, Uttar Pradesh, Jharkhand, Andhra Pradesh, Gujarat and Himachal Pradesh. However in Kerala, Bihar, Assam, Jammu & Kashmir Karnataka, Uttaranchal, Delhi, Maharashtra, Rajasthan, Madhya Pradesh, Tamil Nadu, Orissa, Chattisgarh and Punjab it was somewhat better than SCs/STs.

In the same way, the percentage of those who completed at least Primary School during 2001 at All India level among Muslims was 60.9 compared to 61.4 for SCs/STs and 79.3% for all others. The percentage of Muslim urban males was 71.3 as against 80.2 for SCs/STs and 89.6 for all others and for urban females it was 70.9 in contrast to 74.8 for SCs/STs and 89.6 for all others. For rural males the percentage who completed at least Primary School was 58.9 as against 66.1 for SCs/STs and 80.8 for all others and for rural Muslim females it was 47.8 in comparison to 47.0 for SCs/STs and 67.6 for all others. In almost all the states Muslim males and females both urban and rural were far behind all others. In West Bengal, Uttar Pradesh, Madhya Pradesh and Jharkhand they were far behind SCs/STs but in Kerala, Bihar, Karnataka, Maharashtra, Andhra Pradesh, Gujarat and Tamil Nadu they were slightly better compared to SCs/STs. The picture pertaining to those who completed at least Middle School was more of less the same. Only 40.5% Muslims completed at least Middle School during 2001 in contrast to 41.3% SCs/STs and 62.7% all others. Likewise, 49.6% Muslim urban males and 51.1% Muslim urban females completed at least Middle School compared to 59.8% and 56.3% SCs/ST urban males and females and 76.7% and 76.7% all other urban males and females respectively. Similarly, 37.3% rural Muslim males and 29.4% Muslim rural females completed at least Middle School in contrast to 43.7% and 29.3% rural males and females from SCs/STs and 62.0% and 49.0% rural males and females from others respectively. In West Bengal, Uttar Pradesh, Karnataka, Maharashtra and Gujarat the position of all including urban and rural males as well as females SCs/STs and all others was better compared to total Muslims and Muslim urban males and females. In Kerala, Bihar, Jharkhand, Andhra Pradesh and Tamil Nadu the position of Muslims including Muslim urban males and females was inferior to all others but slightly better than SCs/STs. If we look at the picture of Muslims including both urban males and females who completed at least Matric during 2001, we find that 23.9% Muslims completed at least Matric compared to 21.1% SCs/STs and 42.5% all others. Likewise, 36.1% Muslim urban males and 32.2% Muslim urban females completed at least Matric compared to 42.1% SC/ST urban males and 31.8% SC/ST urban females and 63.0% all other urban males and 57.9% all other urban females respectively. Similarly, 22.0% and 11.2% Muslim rural males and females completed at least Matric in comparison to 24.5% and 10.2% rural SCs/STs males and 41.8% and 23.8% other rural males and females respectively. In West Bengal and Gujarat, Muslims including urban and rural males and females remained behind SCs/STs and all others while in Kerala, Uttar Pradesh, Bihar, Jharkhand, Karnataka, Maharashtra, Andhra Pradesh, Madhya Pradesh and Tamil Nadu, Muslims both urban and rural males and females remained behind all others save the SC/STs. Thus, we find that in matters of gender wise literacy in urban and rural areas too Muslims are generally far behind national average as well as Hindu Upper Castes, Hindu OBCs and other minorities. In many respects they are lagging in comparison to SCs/STs though in some areas they are marginally superior or equal to them.

A Reflection on the Incidents of Poverty in Various Segments

A glance at the poverty level as per Table 8.3 (Sachar Committee Report), reveals that during 2004-05 the urban poverty incidence among Muslims was 38.4 compared to 22.8 for all and 20.4 for all Hindus, 36.4 for Hindu SCs/STs, 25.1 for Hindu OBCs, 8.3 for Hindu general and 12.2 for other Minorities. Likewise, the incidence of rural poverty among Muslims was 26.9 as against 22.7 for all, 22.6 for all Hindus, 34.8 for Hindu SCs/STs, 19.5 for Hindu OBCs, 9.0 for Hindu General and 14.3 for other Minorities. In matters of urban poverty incidence Muslims were inferior to all, all Hindus, Hindu SCs/STs, Hindu OBCs, Hindu General and other Minorities in West Bengal, Uttar Pradesh, Assam, Jammu & Kashmir, Maharashtra, Gujarat and Chhattisgarh. In urban areas of Kerala, Bihar, Jharkhand, Karnataka, Uttaranchal, Delhi, Andhra Pradesh, Rajasthan, Madhya Pradesh, Haryana, Tamil Nadu, Orissa and Punjab they were far behind all, Hindu OBCs, Hindu General and other Minorities save the SCs/STs. In the same way, in matters of rural poverty incidence, Muslims were far behind all, all Hindus, Hindu SCs/STs, Hindu OBCs, Hindu General and other Minorities in West Bengal, Assam, Jammu & Kashmir and Haryana. However, they were slightly better compared to Hindu SCs/STs in Kerala, Uttar Pradesh, Bihar, Jharkhand, Karnataka, Uttaranchal, Maharashtra, Andhra Pradesh, Rajasthan, Madhya Pradesh and Chattisgarh though they were inferior to all, all Hindus, Hindu OBC, Hindu General and other Minorities in these States. If we look at the urban poverty incidence compared over time between 1987-88 and 2004-05 as per Appendix Table 8.5 (Sachar Committee Report), we find that the urban poverty incidence declined among Muslim from 53 in 1987-88 to 44 in 2004-05 compared to 29 from 38 among the total, 27 from 36 from in Hindus, 46 from 55 among Hindu SCs/STs, 22 from 32 among other Hindus and 16 from 27 among all others respectively. The fall in urban poverty incidence among the total as well as all Hindus, Hindu SCs/STs, other Hindus and all others was favorable compared to Muslims in West Bengal, Assam, Gujarat, Haryana, Chhattisgarh and Punjab. The fall in urban poverty incidence

Table 4.4: State level Urban MPCE according to SRCs 2004-05 (current prices)

States	*All*	*Hindus*				*Muslims*	*All others*
		All Hindus	*SCs/STs*	*OBCs*	*General*		
All India	1105	1139	793	955	1469	804	1485
West Bengal	1159	1214	784	1008	1385	748	2585
Kerala	1354	1363	836	1221	1883	1081	1670
Uttar Pradesh	880	976	668	796	1311	662	1405
Bihar	726	768	681	662	1027	559	708
Assam	1131	1113	888	994	1265	1199	1198
Jammu and Kashmir	1115	1323	949	943	1489	991	1572
Jharkhand	1017	1038	681	877	1433	727	995
Karnataka	1138	1201	729	1007	1580	837	1501
Uttaranchal	1028	1033	768	785	1175	753	2657
Delhi	1419	1423	879	985	1788	1051	1924
Maharashtra	1228	1278	934	1061	1548	921	1399
Andhra Pradesh	1091	1134	851	970	1605	803	1195

States	*All*	*Hindus*				*Muslims*	*All others*
		All Hindus	*SCs/STs*	*OBCs*	*General*		
Gujarat	1206	1227	1045	905	1470	875	1754
Rajasthan	945	979	744	871	1262	685	1254
Madhya Pradesh	893	902	599	782	1232	669	1801
Haryana	1183	1155	744	896	1420	1105	2151
Tamil Nadu	1166	1166	739	1123	2311	1020	1355
Orissa	790	795	558	697	1009	785	701
Himachal Pradesh	1422	1487	1151	1116	1658	869	1393
Chhattisgarh	963	956	754	813	1396	590	1545
Punjab	1306	1241	919	961	1483	811	1469
All other States	1309	1294	908	994	1676	1112	1395

Source: Appendix Table 8.2, Sachar Committee Report.

among Muslims was slightly better compared to SCs/STs in Kerala, Uttar Pradesh, Bihar, Jammu & Kashmir, Jharkhand, Uttaranchal, Delhi, Maharashtra, Andhra Pradesh, Rajasthan, Madhya Pradesh, Tamil Nadu, Orissa and Himachal Pradesh though they were worse off compared to the total, all Hindus, other Hindus and other Minorities in these States. In matters of the fall in rural poverty incidence Muslims were worse off in contrast to the total as well as all Hindus, other Hindus and all others in all States of the country. In some states like West Bengal and Assam they were behind SCs/STs, in Jammu & Kashmir, Uttaranchal, Delhi and Haryana they were more or less at par with SCs/STs but they were slightly better in Kerala, Uttar Pradesh, Bihar, Jharkhand, Karnataka, Maharashtra, Andhra Pradesh, Gujarat, Rajasthan, Madhya Pradesh, Tamil Nadu, Orissa, Himachal Pradesh, Chhattisgarh and Punjab.

The poverty level can also be measured from the Mean Per Capita Expenditure. The State level urban MPCE is shown in the Table 4.4.

The figures for 2004-05 as per Appendix Table 8.2 (Sachar Committee Report) reveal that the State level Urban Mean Per Capita Expenditure for Muslims at current prices was lower compared to all, for all Hindus, for Hindu OBCs, for Hindu General and for all others. Likewise, the rural Mean Per Capita Expenditure for Muslims at current prices was lower in comparison to all, for all Hindus, for Hindu OBCs. for Hindu General and for all others save SCs/STs. In matters of Urban Mean Per Capita Expenditure the condition of Muslims was poor compared to all, all Hindus, Hindu SCs/STs, Hindu OBCs, Hindu General and all others in West Bengal, Uttar Pradesh, Bihar, Uttaranchal, Maharashtra, Andhra Pradesh, Gujarat, Rajasthan, Himachal Pradesh, Chattisgarh and Punjab. They were behind all, all Hindus, Hindu OBCs, Hindu General and all others save Hindu SCs/STs in Kerala, Assam, Jammu & Kashmir, Jharkhand, Karnataka, Delhi, Madhya Pradesh, Tamil Nadu and Orissa. As far as the rural Mean Per Capita Expenditure is concerned Muslims were behind all, all Hindus Hindu OBCs, Hindu General and all others except Hindu SCs/STs in West Bengal, Kerala, Uttar Pradesh, Bihar, Assam, Jammu & Kashmir, Jharkhand, Karnataka,

Table 4.5. Percentage of Workers Employed in Manufacturing Sector in each State by SRCs, 2004-05

State	*All*	*Hindu*				*Muslims*			*Others Minorities*
		All Hindus	*SC/STs*	*OBC*	*Upper Castes*	*All Muslims*	*OBC*	*General*	
All India	11.8	11.0	8.7	11.9	12.4	20.5	21.7	19.7	9.0
Andhra Pradesh	10.8	10.1	4.8	13.8	7.9	19.6	15.8	20.5	13.3
Assam	3.6	3.8	3.8	2.7	4.6	2.9	0.7	2.9	7.9
Bihar	6.2	5.3	4.4	6.2	3.1	13.2	14.4	11.2	10.6
Delhi	25.1	21.9	25.9	28.5	18.3	57.9	68.1	55.5	18.7
Gujarat	16.0	16.3	10.6	14.8	24.9	13.3	9.8	15.0	11.3
Haryana	13.2	13.8	10.4	16.2	14.0	5.6	4.4	11.9	6.3
Himachal Pradesh	5.8	5.8	7.0	4.1	5.5	6.7	5.3	7.3	6.7
Jammu & Kashmir	12.3	6.4	7.9	13.3	4.4	16.2	12.8	16.9	9.3
Karnataka	10.1	8.9	8.2	9.4	9.0	20.3	18.4	22.5	11.3
Kerala	14.9	18.0	12.0	22.1	14.3	9.2	9.2	12.5	10.1
Madhya Pradesh	7.8	6.6	5.7	7.5	6.5	28.3	37.4	20.1	7.6

Table 4.5 (contd..)

State	*All*	*Hindu*				*Muslims*			*Others Minorities*
		All Hindus	*SC/STs*	*OBC*	*Upper Castes*	*All Muslims*	*OBC*	*General*	
Maharashtra	12.2	10.5	10.1	12.4	24,8	25.4	24.7	11.6	11.1
Orissa	11.3	11.4	11.6	12.0	9.1	18.0	6.01	9.3	7.3
Punjab	12.9	23.3	23.0	29.6	21.4	19.0	10.7	28.8	7.6
Rajasthan	8.9	7.8	7.6	7.4	9.6	25.3	25.9	24.5	11.9
Tamil Nadu	19.7	19.2	12.0	21.6	19.0	29.8	30.5	20.7	22.1
Uttar Pradesh	12.5	9.5	9.0	9.4	10.4	28.1	29.2	26.2	6.0
West Bengal	16.8	15.8	11.5	17.4	19.4	20.6	26.0	20.5	6.0

Source: Appendix Table 5.6, Sachar Committee Report.

Table 4.6. Percentage of Workers Engaged in Trade in Each State by SRCs, 2004-05(All Workers)

State	*All*	*Hindus*				*Muslims*			*Other Minorities*
		All Hindus	*SCs/ STs*	*OBCs*	*Upper Castes*	*All*	*OBCs*	*General*	
All India	9.1	8.1	4.7	7.7	13.4	16.8	18.2	15.9	9.7
West Bengal	11.7	12.3	7.4	16.4	15.8	10.5	19.7	10.3	6.8
Kerala	12.2	8.4	2.2	9.8	11.4	27.1	27.3	13.0	11.4
Uttar Pradesh	9.4	7.7	4.6	7.0	15.1	16.7	16.3	17.3	44.2
Bihar	8.8	8.2	3.4	10.4	10.1	13.0	13.6	11.9	6.2
Assam	10.1	9.8	8.4	5.0	15.7	11.7	30.5	11.1	3.8
Jammu& Kashmir	7.9	7.3	4.0	9.6	9.0	8.3	2.3	9.6	7.5
Jharkhand	7.6	7.2	2.8	8.5	16.4	8.6	9.7	6.7	1.1
Karnataka	8.4	6.7	4.3	6.6	9.3	22.2	21.4	23.2	17.1
Delhi	24.2	25.1	20.2	20.8	28.6	19.3	0.3	23.7	19.4
Maharashtra	9.5	8.1	6.4	6.8	10.4	23.3	14.6	24.5	10.6
Andhra Pradesh	8.5	7.7	4.0	7.5	12.6	20.0	11.6	21.9	6.7

Table 4.6 (contd..)

State	*All*	*Hindus*				*Muslims*			*Other Minorities*
		All Hindus	*SCs/ STs*	*OBCs*	*Upper Castes*	*All*	*OBCs*	*General*	
Gujarat	8.9	7.3	2.7	6.4	13.8	22.7	24.2	21.9	27.5
Rajasthan	6.7	6.1	4.1	5.0	13.7	12.6	12.7	12.4	13.3
Madhya Pradesh	7.2	5.9	3.2	5.9	13.5	20.1	19.2	21.0	36.0
Haryana	11.1	11.1	10.3	9.6	12.5	13.5	11.1	26.0	10.9
Tamil Nadu	9.5	8.4	5.2	9.2	14.5	37.2	36.2	50.4	14.2
Orissa	7.5	7.4	3.5	9.0	15.0	33.6	52.2	31.7	2.4
Himachal Pradesh	4.7	4.6	1.9	9.4	4.9	8.9	1.9	11.6	2.4
Punjab	11.5	21.3	12.8	15.0	31.1	7.4	8.5	6.2	6.7

Source: Appendix Table 5.7, Sachar Committee Report.

Uttaranchal, Delhi, Maharashtra, Andhra Pradesh, Gujarat, Rajasthan, Madhya Pradesh, Haryana, Tamil Nadu, Orissa, Himachal Pradesh, Chhattisgarh and Punjab.

There are several reasons for poverty among Muslims but among them the most significant are: the low participation of workers especially among womenfolk, meager land holdings, near absence in Government jobs, negligible representation in corporate sector, excessive dependence on artisanship and petty jobs. According to the figures of 2004-05, (Sachar Committee Report, Appendix 5.5), the worker population rates among Muslims was 54.9 compared to 64.4 for all, 65.8 for all Hindus, 71.4 for Hindu SCs/STs, 67.3 for Hindu OBCs, 57.4 for Hindu Upper Castes and 64.5 for other Minorities. Muslims were behind all Hindus, Hindu SCs/STs and Hindu OBCs in Andhra Pradesh, Assam, Bihar, Gujarat, Jammu & Kashmir, Karnataka, Kerala, Madhya Pradesh, Maharashtra, Orissa, Rajasthan, Tamil Nadu and Uttar Pradesh. They were slightly better off in comparison to all Hindus, Hindu SCs/STs and Hindu OBCs in Haryana, Himachal Pradesh and Punjab. Besides, Muslims were mainly engaged in manufacturing sector, trade and as self-employed workers. Table 4.5 reveals the percentage of workers employed in manufacturing sector:

Muslims' percentage employed in manufacturing sector during 2004-05 as per Appendix Table 5.6 (Sachar Committee Report) was 20.5 compared to 11.0 for all Hindus, 8.7 for Hindu SCs/STs, 11.9 for Hindu OBCs, 12.4 for Hindu Upper Castes and 9.0 for other Minorities. In Andhra Pradesh, Bihar, Delhi, Jammu & Kashmir, Karnataka, Madhya Pradesh, Maharashtra, Rajasthan, Tamil Nadu, Uttar Pradesh and West Bengal the percentage of Muslim workers employed in manufacturing sector was larger than that of all Hindus, Hindu SCs/STs, Hindu OBCs and other Minorities. However, in Assam, Gujarat, Haryana, Himachal Pradesh, Kerala and Punjab they were marginally inferior to others.

Likewise, the proportion of Muslims engaged in trade as shown by the Table 4.6 too was significant:

The Table 4.6 statistics show that 16.8% Muslims were engaged in trade during 2004-05 as per Appendix Table 5.7 (Sachar Committee Report) as against 8.1 all Hindus, 4.7 Hindu

Table 4.7.Share of Muslim Population in Selected States, Groupwise

States	*Total number of employees*	*Muslim population %*	*Higher positions*	*Lower positions*	*Group A*	*Group B*	*Group C*	*Group D*	*Others*
West Bengal	134972	25.2	4.7	1.8	6.7	3.9	2.1	2.5	1.4
Kerala	268733	24.7	10.3	10.4	11.8	10.1	11.1	9.1	10.5
Uttar Pradesh	134053	18.5	7.5	4.9	4.6	8.0	4.3	5.4	6.6
Bihar	78114	16.5	7.2	7.6	7.9	7.0	7.3	8.4	5.2
Assam	81261	30.9	10.2	11.4	9.2	10.7	11.5	9.9	10.5
Jharkhand	15374	13.8	3.8	7.2	4.0	3.7	9.0	4.5	-
Karnataka	528401	12.2	4.9	8.9	4.7	5.1	9.3	6.0	-
Delhi	135877	11.7	2.1	3.3	2.5	1.4	3.9	1.1	1.6
Maharashtra	915645	10.6	3.1	4.5	2.3	3.4	4.4	4.6	-
Gujarat	754533	9.1	3.4	5.5	-	-	-	-	-
Tamil Nadu	529597	5.6	4.2	2.9	4.0	4.2	3.1	2.5	-
Sum States	4452851	16.0	5.7	5.6	5.8	6.1	5.9	5.1	3.3

Source: Appendix Table 9.5, Sachar Committee Report.

SCs/STs, 7.7 Hindu OBCs, 13.4 Hindu Upper Castes and 9.7 all other Minorities. Muslims participation rate in trade in Kerala, Bihar, Karnataka, Maharashtra, Andhra Pradesh, Gujarat, Madhya Pradesh, Haryana, Tamil Nadu, and Orissa was greater compared to all Hindus, Hindu SCs/STs, Hindu OBCs, Hindu Upper Castes and other Minorities. It was marginally lower or more or less equal to others in Uttar Pradesh, Assam, Jammu & Kashmir, Jharkhand, Delhi, Rajasthan, Himachal Pradesh and Punjab. In the same way, as per Table Appendix 5.8, in matters of percentage of self-employed workers in urban areas Muslims' percentage was highly significant. 57.4% Muslims from the category of all Muslims were engaged as self-employed workers in comparison to 42.6% all Hindus, 33.4% Hindu SCs/STs, 46.1% Hindu OBCs, 44.0% Hindu Upper Castes and 41.2% other Minorities. Ironically the percentage of self-employed workers among Muslims was higher compared to all Hindus, Hindu SCs, Hindu OBCs, Hindu Upper Castes and other Minorities in West Bengal, Kerala, Utter Pradesh, Assam, Jammu & Kashmir, Karnataka, Delhi, Maharashtra, Andhra Pradesh, Gujarat, Rajasthan, Madhya Pradesh, Tamil Nadu Orissa, Himachal Pradesh and Punjab. Their percentage was slightly lower in Bihar and Haryana. In almost all the states of the country Muslims are mainly engaged as merchants and shopkeepers, sales persons and sales assistants, tailors, dress-makers, transport equipment operators, tobacco preparers, spinners, weavers, knitters, dyers, machinery fitters, bidi workers and mechanics. Their participation in the professional and management cadre is low. They get lower daily earnings in public as well as private jobs and they are more vulnerable due to the absence of written contracts and social security benefits.

Pathetic Conditons in Government Jobs at Micro Level

It is most unfortunate that the share of Muslims in government jobs is highly meager. Table 4.7 shows the share of Muslim employees in selected State Governments:

As per the Table 4.7 (Sachar Committee Report), out of the 44,52,851 employees selected in state governments, 134972 employees were selected in West Bengal out of which Muslims share at higher positions was to the extent of 4.7 %, at lower positions to the tune of 1.8%, at Group A , 6.7%, Group B, 3.9% Group C, 2.1%, Group D, 2.5% and at others 1.4% when the fact is that Muslims constitute 25.2% of the total population. Kerala employed 268733 employees and Muslims constitute 24.7% of the total population but their share at Higher Positions was to the extent of 10.3%, at Lower Positions, 10.4%, at Group A, 11.8%, at Group B, 10.1%, at group C, 11.1%, at Group D, 9.1% and at others 10.5%. Uttar Pradesh absorbed 134053 employees and Muslims despite constituting 18.5% of the total population got 7.5% at Higher Positions, 4.9% at Lower Positions, 4.6% at Group A, 8.0% at Group B, 4.3% at Group C, 5.4% at Group D and 6.7% at others. Bihar engaged 78114 employees and Muslims constitute 16.5% but they got 7.2% at Higher Positions, 7.6% at Lower Positions, 7.9% at Group A, 7.0% at Group B, 7.3% at Group C, 8.4% at Group D and 5.2% at others. Muslims in Assam constitute 30.9% of total population and the state had employed 81261 people but Muslims share at Higher Positions was 10.2%, at Lower Positions 11.45%, at Group A, 9.2%, at Group B, 10.7%, at Group C, 11.5% at Group D, 9.95% and at others 10.5%. Muslim population in Jharkhand is 13.8% and the state had engaged 15374 employees but Muslims share at Higher Positions was 3.8%, at Lower Positions 7.25% at Group A, 4.05%, at Group B, 3.75%, at Group C, 9.0% and at Group D, 4.5%. Karnataka employed 52801 employees and Muslims constitute 12.2% of the total population but Muslims share at Higher Positions was 4.9%, at Lower Positions, 8.9%, at Group A, 4.7%, at Group B, 5.1%, at Group C, 9.3%, and at Group D, 6.0%. Delhi has 11.7% Muslim population and it had employed 135877 employees but Muslims share at Higher Position was 2.1%, at Lower Positions 3.3%, at Group A, 3.5%, at Group B, 1.45%, at Group C, 3.9%, at Group D, 1.1% and at others 1.6%. Maharashtra employed 915645 employees and it has 10.6% Muslim population but Muslims share at Higher Positions was 3.1%, at Lower Positions, 4.5%, at Group A, 2.3%, at Group B, 3.4%, at Group C, 4.4%, at Group D, 4.6% and at others 1.6%. Gujarat has 9.1% Muslim population and it had employed 754533 employees and Muslims share at Higher Positions was 3.4% and at Lower Positions 5.5%. Tamil Nadu has 5.6% Muslim population and Muslims share at

Table 4.8. Share of Muslim Employees in Selected State Government Departments (No. of Employees 44,52,851)

States	*Muslim Population %*	*Education Dept.*		*Home Dept.*		*Health Dept.*		*Transport Dept.*		*Other Dept.*	
		Higher	*Lower*	*Higher*	*Lower*	*Higher*	*Lower*	*Higher*	*Lower*	*Higher*	*Lower*
West Bengal	25.2	-	-	14.1	5.1	1.3	0.9	-	-	4.3	2.2
Kerala	24.7	13.0	11.7	10.8	10.7	11.2	10.2	9.4	9.2	8.9	10.5
Uttar Pradesh	18.5	-	-	8.1	9.9	4.3	5.6	1.9	4.9	7.6	4.8
Bihar	16.5	14.8	11.8	5.9	7.1	-	2.6	8.3	10.9	7.5	7.6
Assam	30.9	-	-	9.3	11.5	8.0	11.1	13.9	11.5	12.2	11.4
Jharkhand	13.8	-	-	5.7	7.6	6.0	3.2	-	-	3.7	7.8
Karnataka	12.2	5.0	12.2	3.6	4.2	4.7	5.0	16.8	7.0	5.1	7.3
Delhi	11.7	5.9	7.2	1.5	2.3	1.0	1.8	1.4	1.1	0.3	09
Maharashtra	10.6	2.9	4.7	4.2	4.2	2.6	3.3	-	-	2.2	3.9
Gujarat	9.1	1.7	4.5	5.6	5.6	2.2	1.5	9.4	16.3	-	-
Tamil Nadu	5.6	5.8	5.3	0.0	2.6	4.6	3.3	1.0	2.6	2.9	2.1
Sum of States	16.0	5.7	6.2	8.7	5.6	4.4	3.5	1.6	6.9	5.5	5.1

Source: Table 9.6, Sachar Committee Report.

Higher Positions was 4.2%, at Lower Positions 2.9%, at Group A, 4.0%, at Group B 4.2%, at Group C, 5.1% and at group D 2.5%. If we take the combined position of all the above 11 states which employed 4452851 employees and in which Muslims constitute on an average 16.0% of the total population of these eleven states, we find that only 5.7% Muslims on an average were employed at Higher Positions, 5.6% at Lower Positions, 5.8% at Group A, 6.1% at Group B, 5.9% at Group C, 5.1% at Group D and 3.3% at others. Nowhere they were employed in proportion to their share in the population. Their major chunk of the Government jobs has been secured by other groups for the last sixty years and only God knows for how long this situation would continue in a democratic country like India where Minorities have been provided several safeguards for their growth and development.

If we now analyze the share of Muslims in various state government departments as per the Table 4.8 (Sachar Committee Report), we find a depressing position.

The Table 4.8 shows that out of 4452851 employees employed by the eleven states, the position in West Bengal with 25.2% Muslim population was that only 14.1% Muslims were employed at Higher Positions and 5.1% at Lower Positions in Home Department. Similarly, 1.3% and 0.9% were employed at Higher and Lower Positions respectively in Health Department and 4.3% and 2.2% at Higher and Lower Positions in other Department respectively. Kerala with 24.7% Muslim population got 13.0% and 11.7% at Higher and Lower Positions respectively in Education Department, 10.8% and 10.7% respectively at Higher and Lower Positions in Home Department, 11.2% and 10.2% respectively at Higher and Lower Positions in Health Department, 9.4% and 9.2% respectively at Higher and Lower Positions in Transport Department and 8.9% and 10.5% respectively at Higher and Lower Positions in other Departments. Uttar Pradesh with 18.5% Muslim population got 8.1% and 9.9%. in Home Department, 4.3% and 5.6% in Health Department, 1.9% and 4.9% in Transport Department and 7.6% and 4.8% in other Departments respectively. Bihar with 16.5% Muslim population had 14.8% and 11.85% at Higher and Lower Positions respectively in Education Department, 5.9% at Higher Positions and 7.1% at Lower Positions in Home Department, 2.6% at Lower Positions, in Health Department, 8.3% and 10.9% in Transport Department at Higher and Lower Positions respectively and 7.5% at Higher positions and 7.6% at Lower Positions in other Departments. Assam with 30.9% Muslim population got 9.3% and11.5%, 8.0% and 11.1%, 13.9% and 11.5%, and 12.2% and 11.4% in Home Department, Health Department, Transport Department and other Department at Higher and Lower Positions respectively. Jharkhand with 13.8% Muslim population obtained 5.7% at Higher Positions and 7.6% at Lower Positions in Home Department, 6.0% and 3.2% at Higher and Lower Positions respectively in Health Department and 3.7% at Higher Positions and 7.8% at Lower Positions in other Departments. Karnataka with 12.2% Muslim population secured 5.0%, 12.4% at Higher and Lower Positions in Education Department respectively, 3.6% at Higher Positions and 4.2% at Lower Positions in Home Department, 4.7% and 5.0% at Higher and Lower Positions respectively in Health Department, 16.8% and 7.0% at Higher Positions and Lower Positions respectively in Transport Department and 5.1% at Higher Positions and 7.3% at Lower Positions in other Departments. Delhi with 11.7% Muslim population engaged 5.9% at Higher Positions and 7.2% at Lower Positions in Education Department, 1.5% and 2.3% at Higher and Lower positions respectively in Home Department, 1.0% at Higher Positions and 1.8% at Lower Positions in Health Department, 1.4% and 1.1 % at Higher and Lower Positions respectively in Transport Department and 0.3% and 0.9% at Higher and Lower Positions respectively in other Departments. Maharashtra having 10.6% Muslim population secured 2.9% and 4.7% Higher and Lower Positions respectively in Education Department, 4.2% at Higher and 4.2% at Lower Positions in Home Department, 2.6% at Higher Positions and 3.3% at Lower Positions in Health Department and 2.2% and 3.9% at Higher and Lower Positions respectively in other Departments. Gujarat possessing 9.1% Muslim population absorbed 1.7% at Higher Positions and 4.5% at Lower Positions in Education Department, 5.6% and 5.6% at Higher and Lower Positions respectively in Home Department, 2.2% at Higher Positions and 1.5% at Lower Positions in Health Department, 9.4% and

16.3% at Higher and Lower Positions respectively in Transport Departments. Tamil Nadu with 5.6% Muslim population engaged 5.8% at Higher Positions and 5.3% at Lower Positions in Education department, 0.0% and 2,6% at Higher and Lower Positions respectively in Home Department, 4.6% at Higher Positions, 3.3% at Lower Positions in Health Department, 1.0% and 2.6% at Higher and Lower Positions respectively in Transport Department and 2.9% and 2.1% at Higher and Lower Positions respectively in other Departments. If we take into consideration the cumulative picture of the eleven states with 16.0% Muslim population, we find that 5.7% Muslims on an average were absorbed in Education Department at Higher Positions and 6.2% at Lower Positions. Similarly, in Home Department 8.7% Muslims were engaged at Higher Positions and 5.6% at Lower Positions. Like wise, in Health Department 4.4% Muslims at Higher Positions and 3.5% at Lower Positions were employed. In the same way, 1.6% Muslims at Higher Positions and 6.9% at Lower Positions were absorbed in Transport Department and 5.5% Muslims at Higher Positions and 5.1% at Lower Positions were employed in other Departments respectively. The department wise picture also shows the poor state of affairs for nowhere Muslims were employed in proportion to their numerical strength. As a matter of fact the data as discussed above which was provided by State Governments pertaining to employment reveals that the total share of Muslims among all types of jobs in West Bengal with 25.2% Muslim population was merely 2.1%, in Kerala with 24.7% Muslim population it was 10.45%, in Uttar Pradesh with 18.5% Muslim population it was 5.1%, in Bihar with 16.5% Muslim population it was 7.6% and in Assam with 30.9% Muslim population it was 11.2%. Similarly, in Jharkhand with 13.8% Muslim population it was 6.7%, in Karnataka with 12.2% Muslim population it was 8.5% and in Delhi with 11.75% Muslim population it was 3.2%. Likewise, in Maharashtra with 10.6% Muslim population it was 4.45, in Andhra Pradesh with 9.2% Muslim population it was 8.8%, in Gujarat with 9.1% Muslim population it was 5.4%, in Tamil Nadu with 5.6% Muslim population it was 3.2% and in the above states taken together with 15.4% Muslim population it was 6.3%.

Table 4.9 Share of Muslim Employees in Judiciary

(Percentages)

States	*Share of Muslim Employees*	*Advocate General*	*Dist Session Judge*	*Addl. Distt. And Session Judge*	*Chief Judicial Magistrate*	*Pri. Judge*	*Munsif*	*Public Prosecutors*	*Group*			
									A	*B*	*C*	*D*
West Bengal	5.0	0.0	4.8	7.7	7.8	0.0	3.2	5.4	2.3	3.4	4.3	7.1
Kerala	12.3	-	-	-	-	-	-	-	9.4	13.0	12.7	12.1
Uttar Pradesh	10.9	3.1	8.4	7.5	0.0	10.7	4.7	8.6	16.0	10.4	11.9	
Assam	9.4	0.0	0.0	12.2	9.5	50.0	15.3	16.8	0.0	0.0	9.0	9.7
Jammu & Kashmir	48.3	51.1	-	42.9	-	0.0	39.7	59.3	59.1	48.8	49.3	-
Karnataka	4.0	-	0.0	6.0	3.4	20.0	2.2	-	2.9	5.3	3.9	4.9
Jharkhand	8.4	0.0	2.9	4.0	0.0	0.0	5.3	0.0	7.4	7.4	8.1	10.4
Uttranchal	3.9	0.0	0.0	0.0	0.0	0.0	12.2	0.0	0.0	3.2	3.8	3.8
Delhi	1.3	-	0.0	0.0	-	-	0.7	-	3.3	0.9	1.0	1.8

Table 4.9 (Contd.)

States	*Share of Muslim Empl-oyees*	*Advocate General*	*Dist Session Judge*	*Addl. Distt. And Session Judge*	*Chief Judicial Magi-strate*	*Pri. Judge*	*Munsif*	*Public Prose-cutors*	*Group*			
									A	B	C	D
Maharashtra	8.1	-	2.3	7.6	8.2	0.0	8.1	6.4	7.5	10.1	7.4	10.7
Andhra Pradesh	12.4	-	1.8	4.3	5.0	-	-	3.1	11.9	12.0	10.9	16.8
Rajasthan	5.1	-	3.0	4.7	2.3	0.0	4.2	-	5.9	5.0	8.9	5.4
Madhya Pradesh	6.0	-	7.2	3.8	6.9	8.3	8.8	-	0.0	3.9	6.8	4.2
Orissa	1.5	-	1.4	-	0.0	0.0	1.8	-	0.0	0.6	1.6	1.5
Chattisgarh	6.9	-	4.2	0.0	4.3	0.0	4.7	100	9.0	0.0	4.5	2.8
Sum States	8.0	20.0	2.7	5.7	5.2	4.3	7.2	7.8	7.7	7.7	7.8	9.0
Exc. J&K	7.8	3.5	2.7	5.5	5.2	4.4	5.8	6.3	6.8	7.1	7.7	9.0

Source: Appendix Table 9.10, Sachar Committee Report.

Employment Situation in Judiciary and Public Sector Undertakings in Selected States

An analysis regarding Muslim employees in Judiciary as per Table 4.9 (Sachar Committee Report), reveals that Muslims' share in various departments pertaining to Judiciary was not satisfactory:

The Table 4.9 exhibits that the share of Muslims in West Bengal in total judicial appointments was to the extent of 5.0%. Out of which there were 4.8% District Session Judges, 7.7% Additional District and Session Judges, 7.8% Chief judicial Magistrates, 3.2% Munsifs, 5.4% Public Prosecutors, 2.3% in Group A, 3.4% in Group B, 4.3% in Group C and 7.1% in Group D. In Uttar Pradesh 10.9% Muslims were employed in the Judiciary and out of which there were 3.1% District Session Judges, 8.4% Additional District and Session Judges, 7.5% Chief Judicial Magistrates, 10.7% Munsifs, 4.7% Public Prosecutors, 8.6% in Group A, 16.0% in Group B, 10.4% in Group C and 11.9% in Group D. In Assam, Muslims share was to the extent of 9.4% out of which Additional District and Session Judges were 12.2%, Chief Judicial Magistrates 9.5%, Prl. Judges 50.0%, Munsifs 15.3%, Public prosecutors16.8%, in Group C 9.0% and in Group D, 9.7%. In Jammu & Kashmir Muslims were appointed to the extent of 48.3% out of which 51.1% were Advocate Generals, 42.9% Additional District and Session Judges, 39.7% Munsifs, 59.3% Public prosecutors, 59.1% in Group A, 48.8% in Group B, and 49.3% in Group C. In Karnataka the share of Muslims in Judiciary was to the tune of 4.0% out of which 6.0% were Additional District and Session Judges, 3.4% Chief Judicial Magistrates, 20.0% Prl. Judges, 2.2% Munsifs, 2.9% in Group A, 5.3% in Group B, 3.9% in Group C and 4.9% in Group D. In Jharkhand, the Muslims share was 8.4% out of which 2.9% were District Session Judges, 4.0% Additional District and Session Judges, 5.3% Munsifs, 7.4% in Group A, 7.4% in Group B, 8.1% in Group C and 10.4% in Group D. In Uttaranchal there were 3.9% Muslim employees out of which 12.2% were Munsifs, 3.2% in Group B, 3.8% in Group C and 3.8% in Group D. In Delhi there were 1.3% Muslims out of which 0.7% were Munsifs, 3.3% in Group A, 0.9% in Group B, 1.o% in Group C and 1.8% in Group D. In Maharashtra the share of Muslims was to the extent of 8.1% out of which

Table 4.10. Share of Muslim Employees in State PSUs (No. of employees: 7,63,4390)

State	*Higher Positions*	*Lower Positions*	*Group A*	*Group B*	*Group C*	*Group D*	*Others*
West Bengal	1.2	6.3	0.0	1.2	6.3	5.1	..
Kerala	9.5	11.1	9.5	9.6	9.3	11.7	..
Uttar Pradesh	6.2	5.3	7.9	5.5	6.4	4.9	7.1
Bihar	8.6	6.4	1.5	11.0	6.6	4.2	11.1
Karnataka	8.6	9.9	7.1	9.2	7.8	14.7	8.4
Delhi	2.1	5.6	0.0	2.2	2.9	6.6	0.0
Maharashtra	1.9	1.1	1.6	3.8	...	1.1	7.9
Gujarat	8.5	16.0	9.9	5.5	16.7	15.4	4.3
Tamil Nadu	3.2	2.6	2.6	3.3	2.6	2.5	-
Sum of States	7.4	9.9	7.2	7.5	9.3	10.9	8.3

Source: Appendix Table 9.11, Sachar Committee Report.

2.3% were District Session Judges, 7.6% Additional District and Session Judges, 8.2% Chief Judicial Magistrates, 8.1% Munsifs, 6.4% Public Prosecutors, 7.5% In Group A, 10.1% in Group B, 7.4% in Group C, and 10.7% in Group D. In Andhra Pradesh, the Muslims were to the tune of 12.4% out of which 5.0% were Advocate Generals, 1.8% District Session Judges, 4.3% Additional District and Session Judges, 5.0 % Chief Judicial Magistrates, 3.1% Public Prosecutors, 11.9% in Group A, 12.0% in Group B, 10.9% in Group C and 16.8% in Group D. In Rajasthan, the share of Muslims was 5.1% out of which 3.0% were District Session Judges, 4.7% Additional District and Session Judges, 2.3% Chief Judicial Magistrates, 4.2% Munsifs, 5.9% in Group A, 5.0% in Group B, 8.9% in Group C and 5.% in Group D. In Madhya Pradesh, Muslims in Judiciary were 6.0% out of which 7.2% were District Session Judges, 3.8% Additional District and Session Judges, 6.9% Chief Judicial Magistrates, 8.3% Prl. Judges, 8.8% Munsifs, 3.95 in Group B, 6.8% in Group C and 4.2% in Group D. In Orissa, the share of Muslims was to the limit of 1.5% out of which 1.4% were District Session Judges, 1.8% Munsifs, 0.6% in Group B, 1.6% in Group C and 1.55% in Group D. In Chhattisgarh there were 6.9% Muslims out of which 4.2% were District Session Judges, 4.3% Chief Judicial Magistrates, 4.7% Munsifs, 10.0% Public prosecutors, 9.0% in Group A, 4.5% in Group C and 2.8% in group D. If we take the average of all among the above fifteen states we find that Muslims share in Judiciary in these states was to the extent of 8.0% out of which 20.0% were Advocate Generals, 2.75% District Session Judges, 5.7% additional District and Session Judges, 5.2% Chief Judicial Magistrates, 4.3% Prl. Judges, 7.2% Munsifs, 7.8% Public prosecutors, 7.7% in Group A, 7.7% in Group B, 7.8% in Group C and 9.0% in group D.

Ironically, the picture with reference to the employment of Muslims in PSUs too was miserable as is visible from Table 4.10 (Sachar Committee report):

From the Table 4.10 figures it is quite apparent that out of 7,63,439 employees Muslims share in West Bengal at Higher Positions was 1.2%, at Lower Positions 6.3%, in Group B 1.2%, in Group C 6.3% and in Group D, 5.1%. In Kerala, it was 9.5% at Higher Positions, 11.1% at Lower Positions, 9.5% in Group A, 9.6% in Group B, 9.3% in Group C and 11.7% in Group D.

In Uttar Pradesh, it was 6.2% at Higher Positions, 5.3% at Lower Positions, 7.9% in Group A, 5.5% in Group B, 6.4% in Group C, 4.9% in Group D and 7.1% in others. In Bihar, it was 8.6% at Higher Positions, 6.4% at Lower Positions, 1.5% in Group A, 11.0% in Group B, 6.6% in Group C, 4.2% in Group D and 11.1% in others. In Karnataka, it was 8.6% at Higher Positions, 9.0 % at Lower Positions, 7.1% in Group A, 9.2% in Group B, 7.8% in Group C, 14.7% in Group D and 8.45 in others. In Delhi, it was 2.15 at Higher Positions, 5.6% at Lower Positions, 2.2% in Group B, 2.9% in Group C and 6.6% in Group D. In Maharashtra, it was 1.9% at Higher Positions, 1.1% at Lower Positions, 1.6% in Group A, 3.8% in Group B, 1.1% in Group D and 7.9% in others. In Gujarat, it was 8.5% at Higher Positions, 16.0% at Lower Positions, 9.9% in Group A, 5.5% in Group B, 16.7% in Group C, 15.4% in Group D and 4.35% in others. In Tamil Nadu, 3.2% were at Higher Positions, 2.65% at Lower Positions, 2.6% in Group A, 3.3% in Group B, 2.6% in Group C and 2.5% in Group D. In the sum total of the nine states we find that there were on an average 7.4% Muslims at Higher Positions, 9.9% at Lower Positions, 7.2% in Group A, 7.5% in Group B, 9.3% in Group C, !0.9% in Group D and 8.3% in others. In this case also Muslims failed to capture their share in proportion to their population in these nine states.

Poor and Inadequate Infrastructure

Muslims are mostly handicapped in getting educational, health, communication and transport facilities. More than 1000 Muslim concentration villages in West Bengal and Bihar did not have any educational institutions. In Uttar Pradesh this figure was to the extent of 1943. Similarly, a large number of Muslim concentration villages in West Bengal, Uttar Pradesh, Bihar, Assam, Jammu & Kashmir and Jharkhand lacked Bus-Stops and Post and Telegraph facilities. Table 4.11 (Sachar Committee Report) shows the number of small, medium and large villages with < 9%, 10-39% and 40% + Muslim population without basic facilities in West Bengal, Uttar Pradesh, Bihar and Assam. However, for convenience sake we have picked up only the Large villages inhabited by 2000 people with 40% + Muslim population without basic facilities in the Table 4.12:

Table 4.11. Number of villages without basic facilities.

Facilities	*Village having more than 2000 population and 40% plus Muslims*
West Bengal	
Education	70
Medical	849
Post	1272
Bus Stop	1846
Proper Approach Road	1124
Uttar Pradesh	
Education	158
Medical	1240
Post	850
Bus Stop	2144
Proper Approach Road	488
Bihar	
Education	100
Medical	1208
Post	910
Bust stop	1386
Proper Approach Road	866
Assam	
Education	8
Medical	698
Post	767
Bus Stop	652
Proper Approach Road.	596

Source: Appendix Table 7.1, Sachar Committee Report.

From Table 4.11 it is apparent that there were 70 large villages having more than 2000 population with more than 40% Muslim population without education, 849 without medical, 1272 without Post Offices, 1846 without Bus -Stops and 1124 without proper Approach roads in West Bengal. In Uttar Pradesh there were 158 large villages with more than 40% Muslim population without education, 1240 without medical, 850 without Post and Telegraph, 2144 without bus-stops and 488 without proper approach roads. Bihar had 100 large villages with more than 40% Muslim population without education, 1208 without medical, 910 without post and Telegraph, 1386 without bus-stops and 866 without proper approach roads. Assam too was slightly better. It had 8 large villages with more than 40% Muslim population without education, 698 without medical, 767 without Post and Telegraphs, 652 without bus-stops and 596 without approach roads. As a general rule Muslim concentration villages both at the rural and urban areas are found without access to the basic facilities. For instance, the proportion of Muslim households living in pucca houses is far less compared to the total population. Compared to the Muslim dominated areas, the areas inhabiting fewer Muslims had better roads, sewage and drainage and water supply facilities. In the same way, their position in matters of availability of piped- water, electricity and modern fuel is miserable compared to other sections of the society.

Starving Financial Conditions at Grass Root Level

If we glance at the financial side of the Muslim community, we find that in matters of priority sector advances of ASC Bs for five years' ending 31st March 2000 to 31st March 2005 Muslims share in amount outstanding was 4.6% compared to 6.6% for other Minorities and 88.9% for others. Likewise, in matter of amount outstanding per account of all Scheduled Commercial Banks for 5 year's ending 31st March 2001-2005 it was Rs.22542 as against Rs. 47546 for other Minorities, Rs 66304 for others and Rs. 59420 for all. Similarly, the percentage share of Muslims in matters of amount outstanding in priority sector advances for Scheduled Commercial Banks by economic classification for 3 years ending 31st March 2002-2005 was 5.2% in agriculture, 5.2% in Small Scale industries and 5.9%

in other priority sectors. In the same way, as per the Table 4.12 (Sachar Committee Report), the share of Muslims in individual deposits in Scheduled Commercial banks by state for 3 years ending March 2002-2005 was Negligible.

Table 4.12: Share of Muslims in individual Deposit in Scheduled Commercial Banks by state Annual Average for 3 years ending 31st March 2002-March 2005.

State	*Percentage Share of Muslims in*	
	No. of Accounts	*Amount*
West Bengal	12.1	5.5
Kerala	17.6	15.3
Uttar Pradesh	7.4	8.5
Bihar	8.7	13.3
Assam	5.5	5.1
Jammu & Kashmir	31.8	30.2
Jharkhand	5.5	8.0
Karnataka	6.2	7.6
Uttaranchal	4.3	7.7
Delhi	2.6	3.9
Maharashtra	8.1	8.6
Andhra Pradesh	5.4	6.2
Gujarat	7.6	8.9
Rajasthan	7.5	7.4
Madhya Pradesh	8.3	6.1
Haryana	1.8	1.6
Tamil Nadu	4.9	6.5
Orissa	4.4	4.8
Himachal Pradesh	2.5	2.2
Chhattisgarh	9.2	9.6
Punjab	1.8	1.4
Others	3.5	2.2
All States	7.6	7.4

Source: Appendix Table 6.7, Sachar Committee Report.

The Table 4.13 indicates that Muslims share in matters of the number of accounts and amounts at the level of all States was 7.6% and 7.4% respectively. For West Bengal in matters of amounts it was 5.5%, Kerala, 15.35%, Uttar Pradesh 8.5%, Bihar 13.3%, Assam 5.1%, Jammu & Kashmir 30.2%, Jharkhand 8.0%, Karnataka, 7.6%, Uttaranchal 7.7%, Himachal Pradesh 2.2%, Delhi 3.9%, Maharashtra 8.6%, Andhra Pradesh 6.2%, Gujarat 8.9%, Rajasthan 7.4%, Madhya Pradesh 6.15, Haryana 1.6%, Tamil Nadu 6.5%, Orissa 4.8%, Himachal Pradesh 2.2%, Chattisgarh 9.65%, Punjab 1.4% and others 2.2%. Out of the total amount numbering Rs. 31805.29 crores, Muslims were sanctioned merely Rs 179.54 crores or 0.56% by SIDDBI under benefits accruing to Muslims under Programme Implemented during 2000-01 to 2005-06. However, only Rs. 26592 crores were disbursed in total out of which Muslims share in the amount disbursed was Rs. 124.12 crores or just 0.46% of the total amount. Likewise, Muslims share in refinance of Production Credit and Investment Credit during 2004-5 and 2005-6 by NABARD was 3.2% for Production Credit and 3.9% for Investment Credit. Thus, we find that the share of Muslims in the amount outstanding is just 4.7% in contrast to 6.5% for other Minorities which is disproportionate to their respective population share. On an average the amount outstanding per account for Muslims is slightly more than half of that of other Minorities and one-third of others. As a matter of fact as the share of Muslims increases in the population their share in amount outstanding tends to decrease. It is quite interesting to note that the RBI has tried to extend banking facilities to the Minorities under the 15-point programme but Muslims remained the most handicapped as most of the benefits accrued to other Minorities. Ironically some banks in the country have identified a number of Muslims concentration areas as negative zones where bank credit and other facilities are not easily provided. Muslims are not averse to banking. They need bank credit urgently as most of them are self-employed people. Actually the inadequate targeting and lack of proper planning has led to the failure to address the financial problems of Muslims. Efforts should be made to create awareness among Muslims about various schemes of the banks impartially and transparently and steps should be taken to specifically direct credit to Muslims along with getting the necessary information about the disbursement and the success of various schemes of the banks.

Condition of Muslim OBCs

Muslims too have OBCs and STs. According to thc figures of 2004-05 there were 0.8% Muslim SCs, 0.5% Muslim STs, 39.2% Muslim OBCs and 59.5% others. Many Muslim OBCs believe that they are a socially and economically differentiated group hence they too should be reflected in each and every programme of the Government. Similarly, SCs from among Muslims too are trying to get them included in the category of Scheduled Castes but so far they have not succeeded. Incidentally, 99.74% Muslims in Lakshadweep have been declared as STs. It is interesting to note that the Havanur Commission had recommended reservation to distinct category of a minority group in 1972 not exceeding 6%. Mandal Commission too has listed at least 82 different social groups among Muslims in the OBC list. Muslim caste groups have been generally included by several States either in the OBC or in the MBS list depending upon their socio-economic conditions. Kerala and Karnataka governments have provided reservation to entire Muslim population considering them as backwards. A separate share of 10% was fixed for Muslims in Kerala which was later on increased to 12%. Tamil Nadu Government too has included nearly 95% Muslims within the fold of backward classes though it has done away reservation on ground of religion. There are many Muslim groups from among the backward classes that have found their place in the lists of the States but are missing in the Central list. Similarly, there are many who are in the list of the centre but missing in the States lists.

A Comparitive Situation of Hindu OBCS and Muslim OBCs

Just as our observation in the previous chapter had revealed that the general Muslims were worse off compared to general Hindus the ensuing figures show that Muslim OBCs too are more deprived in comparison to Hindu OBCs practically in every field. Table 4.13 shows the relative position of Hindu OBCs and Muslim OBCs in matters of levels of education:

Table 4.13: Distribution of persons aged 6+ years in each SRCs Levels of Education

(Percentage)

Educational Level	*H-OBCs*	*M-OBCs*
Illiterates	33.4	37.4
Just Literate	1.2	2.9
Below Primary	0.8	1.5
Primary	15.9	17.5
Middle	16.0	16.0
Secondary	15.0	13.1
Higher Secondary	7.4	5.1
Diploma/Certificate	3.9	2.5
Graduate and above	3.2	1.9

Source: Table 10.5, Sachar Committee Report.

From the above Table it is clear that Muslim OBCs are more illiterates in comparison to Hindu OBCs and they are far behind Hindu OBCs in matters of getting education at the level of Secondary, Higher Secondary and Graduation level and above as well as in obtaining Diplomas and Certificates. Their figures are marginally better at the level of just literate, below primary and primary though at Middle they are equal to each other. The work participation rate among Muslim OBCs is about 55% when for Hindu OBCs it is 67%. Likewise, their salary levels both for males and females in public sector and private sector are lower compared to Hindu OBCs.

Table 4.14: Representation in Public Employment

Department / Undertaking / Institution	*H-OBCs*	*M-OBCs*
Central Security Agencies	11.4	3.6
Railway	9.3	0.4
Central PSU	8.3	0.6
SPSC-Recommended for Selection	27.0	0.9
University Faculty	17.6	1.4
University-Non-Teaching	24.9	1.7

Source: Table 10.10, Sachar Committee Report.

Table 4.14 shows their relative representation in public employment.

From the Table 4.14 it is quite clear that Muslim OBCs stand nowhere in comparison to Hindu OBCs in matters of representation in various departments, undertakings and institutions of the government. Practically their presence is nil. Their average monthly per capita expenditure at urban and combined level is lower at Rs. 689 and Rs. 605 compared to Rs.833 and Rs. 620 for Hindu OBCs. They are marginally better off at Rs. 566 compared to Rs. 548 for Hindu OBCs at the rural level. The low representation of Muslim OBCs in practically every sector reveals that they have not taken the advantage of reservation provided to them under the category of backward classes.

Role of Wakfs and Charities

It is heartening to know that many charitable institutions of Muslims run educational institutions through their charities. Islam makes it obligatory on the part of haves to spare some portion of their resources for the have-nots in the shape of Zakat, *fitras*, charities and *sadqas*. Muslims have nearly 4.9 lakh registered Wakfs which are meant for the betterment of poor and needy Muslims but they are mismanaged and are in critical condition. Unfortunately the current annual income from these Wakfs comes to 2.7 per cent. Encroachment of the Wakf property is very common. The following gazetted Wakf properties were in unauthorized possession of Governments and their agencies during 2005-06:

Table 4.15: Wakf Properties

State	*Number of Wakf Properties*
Delhi	316
Rajasthan	60
Karnataka	42
Madhya Pradesh	53
Uttar Pradesh	60
Orissa	53

Source: Box 11.2, Sachar Committee Report.

The Wakfs have the potentials to serve the religious and charitable institutions of Muslims effectively provided they are protected from the encroachments from the government and private agencies and run on commercial principles. There is a need of strict monitoring of the Wakf management and the vacation of encroached lands particular in the possession of various agencies of Central and State Governments. Many state Governments have not paid huge amounts due to the Wakf for the last several years due to one reason or other. There is an urgent need to provide effective legislative, administrative and judicial priorities to Wakfs in order to manage the five lakhs Wakf properties spread throughout the country.

In the end we can conclude that in matters of implementation of programmes and better participation of the community in development and governing process through inclusive development process, the Central and State Governments have failed miserably, Neither the equity and equality of opportunities were ensured, nor justice was done nor the perception of discrimination was eliminated. Since the Muslims feel aggrieved, efforts should be made on priority basis by the state machinery to develop an effective mechanism supported by a well-guarded legal system so that the complaints of discrimination and grievances of the deprived groups may be addressed expeditiously both at the all India and all states levels. It is most unfortunate that many meaningful people suggest that instead of reservation Muslims should be given special facilities in the form of scholarship, coaching and hostel facilities to boost their education. There are several Muslims who too have begun to consider education as the only panacea for Muslims growth and development forgetting the fact that the problems of Muslims are far more complex and intriguing. It is the general belief of majority of Muslims that those who suggest that Muslims should not seek or should not be given the benefits of reservation in Government jobs and educational institution are not the true friends and well-wishers of Muslims. Many questions are raised pertaining to their sincerity and integrity. First of all, why they did not pursue this policy for SCs/STs and the Backward Classes if it was an effective strategy? Secondly, they are supposed to know that it is very difficult for poor Muslims to get professional and technical as well as general education which has become very costly. Thirdly, if they are being provided third class education in ill-equipped government or private or charitable institutions, it would be a great disservice to them. After attending few years of schooling they would at most pass or get third or second division which would block all chances of their future entry in any job market. Their condition would be miserable. On the one hand, they would not get any Government or private job and on the other hand they would become redundant for the profession or stream from which they came. For instance, the son of a carpenter after getting third class would be unfit in the national and international job market and he would not like to go back to his ancestral profession after few years' of schooling. Fourthly, the income inequalities in the country have become very sharp. There are billionaires and millionaires as well as poor and paupers across various sections of the country. It would be futile to think that the poor would be able to compete with the rich who get their education in world class schools, colleges, universities and technical and professional institutions. Fifthly, there are various generations in the majority community which are there in the field of education for the last several decades and to expect that the first generation Muslims would be able to compete with them is nothing but something impossible. Over and above this, Muslim society would face an extreme type of disequilibrium vis- a- vis males and females in the job and marriage markets. Since girls are more serious and studious and many employers have soft corners for them in job markets, they are most likely to outnumber boys in the job market. For all practical purposes they would not like to marry those Muslims who would be technicians or petty businessmen, but those who have some lucrative government or private jobs which would be a tough task. This type of situation has arisen in many areas in Rajasthan and a few more states where girls have acquired higher education and they are not finding husbands suiting to their status. Besides this, there seems to be a bias operating in many educational institutions and various job markets including the governing structure which would dent the chances of competent Muslims in educational institutions and job markets. People normally appoint 'their own or known' and hardly give preference to others. The experience of the last sixty years reveals that Muslims by themselves could neither come in adequate number in schools and colleges nor in the job markets due to their own weak background as well as lack of state patronage. It would certainly be difficult for them to succeed in the future too without a well thought out plan. The irony of fate is that there are very few Muslims even in lower grades. For Grade A, B and C one can say that Muslims were not available as they were not qualified and could not compete in various competitive examinations. However, there were Muslims in large number who could be appointed under category D as peons, daftries, kitchen attendants, gardeners but they remained conspicuous by their absence because the general atmosphere in the country was not conducive to them.

There is a near unanimity within the Muslim community that admissions in educational institutions and jobs in government sector are the two aspects which are most vital for their overall development. Once they succeed in these areas their other problems would be solved automatically. Muslims are more than convinced that by themselves they cannot compete with the advanced sections of the country in obtaining admissions in schools, colleges, universities and professional and technical institutions. Likewise, they are more than sure that in the job market also it is next to impossible for them to compete and secure jobs in proportion to their numerical strength with majority fellows who have gone too far ahead of them during the last sixty years. They are of the view that these two fronts can be tackled only when Muslims are provided reservation in educational institutions and in government jobs as has been done in the case of SCs/STs and the Backward Classes. Once they reach the break-even point, these facilities may be withdrawn from them since after that stage they would be able to compete in the open market themselves and would not need any further help in the shape of special privileges from the government.

The misfortune of the Muslim community is that there is a hard core political section in the country which is not willing to give any kind of reservation to Muslims. They claim that reservation purely on the basis of religion cannot be given to Muslims since it is against the Constitution. When it is said to them that reservation to backward Muslims is permissible under the Indian Constitution, they bring the plea that religion-based reservations or concessions are bound to create separatist tendencies among the minorities and they have the potentials to further divide the country on communal lines as has happened in 1947. Besides, there are many people in every political party across the country who despite the party thinking in favour of reservation, sabotage the process of reservation for Muslims within their party forums. In the same way, there are very few takers of the reservation idea in the media, judiciary and bureaucracy. When it comes to giving reservation to Backward Muslims or Scheduled Castes and Scheduled Tribes out of the quota of SCs/STs and Backward Classes, it is vehemently opposed by the SCs/STs and the Backward Classes on the plea that it would usurp their rights. These backward sections have no problem if reservation to Muslims is provided exceeding the 50% limit which is vehemently opposed by the Higher Castes stating that it would violate the Supreme Court dictates. It is because of this that several parties make loud noises at the time of elections but when they come in power keep the issue of reservation of Muslims in the cold storage. What to talk of reservation, even the opening of any educational institution such as a college or a university for the Minorities is opposed by several political parties. When the UPA Government thought of providing educational facilities to minorities especially the Muslims after the publication of Sachar Committee Report by opening a few universities under the patronage of University Grants Commission, it was fiercely opposed by the dominant right wing political parties. Similarly, when the same idea was mooted through Maulana Azad Educational Foundation to avoid the criticism, the same political parties stood as a rock and the government had to abandon the idea due to the pressure of right wing parties. Finally, the ruling government took an unprecedented step against the Act, Statutes and Ordinances of the Aligarh Muslim University by opening a few Centers of Aligarh Muslim University in certain Muslim dominated areas to convince the Muslims that the Government was committed to their cause, though this step of Government too was opposed by a large section of the people and the well-wishers of Aligarh Muslim University throughout the country as being against the interest and contrary to the very spirit of Aligarh Muslim University.

It will not be out of place to mention here that there is a small section of people among Muslims who too believes that Muslims can survive only through their own efforts rather than through the help and assistance from the governing structure. However, the large section of the community including the intellectuals and meaningful people believe that without reservation Muslims cannot achieve their due and they would drift from bad to worse. In view of these difficulties, the issue of reservation for Muslims has become a bone of contention. Since no ruling party possesses the absolute majority in order to take any decisive step, the matter would hang in balance till the right wing parties agree to the idea or the willing party acquires the absolute majority or, consensus is achieved among the majority parties in the country in favour of reservation for backward and downtrodden sections of Muslims. Unfortunately there is a sense of frustration among Indian Muslims. They strongly feel that their voice is not heard at the top levels of the Central and State Governments because neither they have any spokes-persons nor Muslim leadership worth the name. Most of them find them without friends and supporters in the country. Their irony of fate is that despite forming a large section of Indian population they cannot electorally influence the course of event in their favour because they are scattered throughout the country. Save a few constituencies in certain states from where they can win a few seats, they are not in a position to win in a significant manner commensurate to their population share on the basis of Muslim support. Consequently, they have to depend upon majority support which they generally do not get due to polarization of votes on communal lines. In retaliation to it they either try to defeat the candidates of those parties who are against them by supporting the winning candidates against them in order to dent their presence on the national scene or support those parties which they consider as lesser evils. Recently we have observed that Muslims have become politically conscious. They are bitter about their state of affairs as depicted by the Sachar Committee Report. They are not willing to be used as the stooges in the hands of vested political parties. They now want quid pro quo. We find that they are floating their own secular political parties to garner Muslim and likeminded non-Muslim votes. In Assam the party headed by Badruddin Ajmal has won several seats and the Indian Muslim League in Kerala too has emerged as victorious. Similar combinations and associations are being formed in West Bengal, Uttar Pradesh, Bihar, Karnataka and Maharashtra. There are people in the country who are not happy to observe such healthy and secular trends for they consider them against national interest forgetting the fact that there are various religious and caste groups other than Muslims in the country who have formed their own secular or religious parties to protect their political interests. Actually, there is a general bias against Muslims in the country due to terror attacks and the overall poor image of a few radical Muslims in the world which is causing much damage to Indian Muslims despite the fact that most of the Muslims are as good or bad Indians as others are. The encouraging thing is that the UPA Government and various State Governments headed especially by the Backward Classes people or Communists have become sympathetic towards the cause of Muslims especially the backward and marginalized sections of Muslims. It is heartening to note that that the UPA Government had constituted the National Commission for Religious and Linguistic Minorities under the chairmanship of Justice Ranganath Misra to suggest measures for the welfare of socially and economically backward sections among religious and linguistic minorities. Just as we have shown that Muslims are lagging practically in every sector and they cannot come out of the rut without providing them adequate reservation, the Misra Commission too concluded that Muslims were under-represented and sometimes wholly unrepresented in almost all the sectors of Indian economy. Moved by Muslims pathetic conditions and to do justice to the marginalized sections of Muslims, it recommended reservation for backward Muslims in all educational Institutions and government posts to all cadres and grades under the Central and State Governments as has been done for SCs/STs and the backward Classes. The Recommendations of the Commission which have been discussed in the next chapter, if accepted in toto, would go a long way to ameliorate the conditions of Muslims.

5

Reservation for Weaker Sections of Muslims in Education and Government Employment and Modalities for its Implementation

In the light of what we have discussed before we can safely conclude that it appears that despite the claim by the government that it has done much for the Muslims, the facts and figures reveal an entirely different picture. The study convincingly proves that Muslims have been benefited the least by different policies and programmes undertaken by the Central and the State Governments for the betterment of the general public, weaker sections of societies and the minorities since their condition is becoming bad to worse day by day. We have also shown the comparative picture of Muslims vis-a-vis Scheduled Castes, Scheduled Tribes and the Backward Classes to emphasize the fact that they are worse off compared to the other segments in almost all the parameters of growth. One can safely conclude from what we have discussed in details that leaving Muslims as they are would ruin their future. Since by themselves they would not be able to compete and acquire their share in the national pool in the highly competent environment of the country in proportion to their numerical strength. We have also convincingly proved that the Scheduled Castes and the Scheduled Tribes which were the most backward sections of the society due to their exploitation during the last several centuries have gained tremendously in the field of education and have become dominant castes in the governing sector merely due to reservations. In matters of Backward Classes our observation has been that they despite being neglected and ignored over years had marked their presence practically in every field of national renaissance only due to reservation. We have also emphasized that a debate was going on in the country in which majority of Muslims of all shades and colours were bent upon demanding reservation especially in the field of education and government jobs on the pattern of SCs/STs and Backward Classes. Besides, we have hinted here and there that there is near unanimity among the large sections of Muslims that they are being discriminated, neglected, excluded and despised practically in every field of national reconstruction. There is despondency, lethargy and frustration in the community due to the false promises of the ruling governments, lack of support from the opposition political parties and meekness and near absence of Muslim leadership. However, we have found that there is a sea change in the perception and mindset of the young generation of Muslims in the sense that after nearly sixty years of dogmatic slumber they are not raising the bogies of Madarsa teachers, grave yards, Wakf properties, excesses by paramilitary forces but demanding education facilities, jobs and healthy and viable infrastructure to improve their depleted surroundings. They vigorously complain that the process of growth and development is not all-inclusive, they fearlessly emphasize that there is practically no space for them in governing structure and they convincingly stress that no meaningful efforts have been made to bring them within the mainstream. They are firm in their views that they are grappling with the issues of identity, security, equity, growth and integration. They are serious in their resolve that they want to preserve their social, cultural and religious identities and they are also clear in their vision that they need equity and equality of opportunity as well as inclusion in the pluralistic society. They are not disheartened but strongly believe that that the perception of discrimination would be eliminated from their mental canvas and they would become the intrinsic part of the diverse and mosaic culture of vibrant India.

An Overview of Muslim's General State of Affairs

The facts and figures given in the previous chapters also reveal that Muslims are worse off in the field of education which is the main source of social, economic, political and cultural empowerment. Muslim children not only exhibit consistently lower levels of Mean Years of Schooling but most of them revert back to illiteracy within 4-5 years after leaving schools. Muslims have failed to take the benefit of explosion of knowledge in the country since as many as 25 per cent Muslim children in the 6-14 age group have either never attended schools or have left schools due to paucity of funds. The drop-out rate among Muslims at the levels of Primary, Middle and Higher Secondary is higher compared to rest of the communities including SCs and STs. Not only the disparity in attainment of graduation and post graduation degrees and technical and super-technical skills was found widening between Muslims and the rest of the segments of the society since 1970, the probability of Muslims completing graduation was the lowest in comparison to others. Besides, not only one out of the 25 Under-Graduate students and one out of the 50 Post-Graduate students is a Muslim in premier colleges but the unemployment among Muslim graduates is the highest. Most unfortunate thing is that expansion of educational opportunities since Independence has not led to the convergence of attainment levels but the gap between Muslims and others is increasing as the level of education is increased. Muslims lament that the condition of Urdu schools is miserable since no efforts have been made to provide education to Muslim children in their Mother tongue and no measures have been taken to remove the distortions from the text books. They also grieve that the advantage which the Scheduled Castes and Scheduled Tribes have taken of various educational policies, programmes and schemes after Independence through affirmative actions was denied to Muslims despite their persisting in the miserable conditions.

It is true that the engagement in gainful employment is highly essential for every household as it provides purchasing power for buying goods, services, necessities and comforts as well as the luxuries of life and accords the status and dignity in the society and insures the family from future eventualities. However, when we looked at the economic conditions of Muslims, we observed that Muslims were not only relatively more poor both in the urban and rural areas compared to general Hindus, Hindu Upper Castes, Hindu OBCs, other Minorities and even the SCs/STs in many segments, but the poverty gaps between them and others too was increasing with the accelerated growth in the country. In addition to it we also found that a respectable position within the field of industry, trade and commerce is a dream for them, professional, technical, judicial and bureaucratic services are beyond their reach and they are conspicuous by their absence in multinational companies. We found that they were generally occupied in self-employed manufacturing and trade activities. The males in urban areas were mostly engaged as merchants and shopkeepers, sales persons and shop assistants, transport equipment operators, spinners, weavers, knitters and dyers, machinery fitters, assemblers, carpenters and bricklayers. The women were usually busy as tailors, dress makers and tobacco preparers. We also observed that the work participation rate, which is the basic source of earning was lowest among Muslims both men and women in rural as well as urban areas compared to others. Thus, we came to the conclusion that economically Muslims were certainly a deprived lot.

It is also the fact of life that the sharing of meaningful and respectable jobs in governing sector enhance the prestige of every community and give it a sense of participation in the governing structure. Unfortunately all the statistics at our command showed that Muslims presence in the government sector was abysmally very low at all levels. What to talk of secretaries, district magistrates, high court and supreme court judges, superintendents of police and income tax, sales tax and customs officers as well as engineers, doctors, professors and scientists, they were not found in adequate numbers as peons, drivers, kitchen attendants, security guards and police constables. One could notice some IAS, IPS, IFS officers here and there. Likewise, a few station house officers, teachers, doctors, clerks, nurses and station masters might be spotted at the middle level. However, Muslims never confronted their fellow beings in proportion to their numerical strength in any sector of the government. Muslims generally felt alienated when they visited government offices, police stations, educational institutions and commercial organizations since they observed least number of Muslims there. In a pluralistic culture and a vibrant democracy the near absence of any community in every segment of the government is most fatal because it inadvertently gives the impression as if the state is discriminating with its own people.

In the same way, it is quite natural that if some segments of the society live in the posh areas with clean environment, excellent sanitary and health conditions, fine roads, pure water, uninterrupted electric supply and beautiful mansions and others live in the filthy atmosphere, dirty surrounding, depleted roads, polluted water, poor sanitary conditions and ghettos, it does not augur well for any living democracy in the world. It has been observed on large scale that Muslims are mostly concentrated in areas with poor infrastructural facilities. This is affecting their mindset, perception, thinking and access to basic services provided by modern civilization. It is an admitted fact that physical access to education, health, communication and transport services is an integral part of the welfare of any household. However, it is most unfortunate that fearing for their safety, many segments of Muslims have settled in ghettos which have made them easy targets of neglect by Municipal Corporations and civil authorities. Safe drinking water, all-weather roads, regular electric supply, sanitary conditions, better schools, well-equipped hospitals and banks are conspicuous by their absence in Muslim localities. Muslims mostly complain that whenever any new Muslim locality comes into existence, the government plants a police post and not schools, hospitals and recreation parks. Similarly, the villages with large Muslim population too suffer from poor physical and social infrastructure. There appears to be an inverse correlation between the proportion of Muslim population and the availability of infrastructural facilities. Almost half the Muslim households in India lack the access to toilet facilities and in urban areas the proportion of Muslim households using flush toilets is much lower than the proportion for the whole urban population. Muslims and SCs/STs generally live in villages that are considered as least electrified. As the level of electrification increases, their share declines. The disadvantage is larger in Muslim concentration villages because the share of villages with no electricity increases substantially with increase in number of Muslims. Likewise, a marked deficit in matters of tap water in Muslim concentration villages is a reality. Muslim households have least access to tap water compared to others. Similarly, Muslim household use negligible amount of modern fuel such as LPG, electricity or kerosene and the use of such items generally decreases with the increase in the Muslim population and the size of the village. Muslims seem to be at par with SCs/STs and OBCs in matters of house structure but in so many other respects they are worse off and need policy initiatives to ameliorate their worsening conditions.

Finance is the backbone of every society. Money circulates in the society like blood in human body. Just as the lack of blood creates paralysis in human body, similarly the lack of money in any segment paralyze the functioning of that segment. Unfortunately Muslims have also starved financially which has adversely affected their destiny. As we know Muslims are mostly self-engaged people and self-employment in home-based work is the main source of their income. To empower them economically, it is vital that they should be assured of the smooth, adequate and timely supply of credit. However, the ground reality is that not only the flow of credit to Muslims is quite limited but the access of Muslims to public sector and private sector banks as well as specialized institutions such as SIDBI and NABARD is meager. Their financial exclusion has adversely affected their educational, social and economic development. There are several reasons for this malady. Firstly, the lower demand for credit could be due to low income level of the community. Secondly, many Muslims do not know about credit schemes by the banks as several bank officials do not show transparency in publishing such schemes. Thirdly, there are bank officials who do not consider Muslims credit worthy due to their weak financial background and hence they exclude many such Muslims from the purview of the banks. Lastly, there is no dearth of people who are biased against Muslims at implementation stage as a consequence of which very few branches of banks have been opened in minority concentration areas.

The above description convincingly exhibits that after sixty years Muslims have more or less come exactly to that stage where SCs, STs and the OBCs were at the time of 1947. Not only they are depressed, resource less and jobless but there is a feeling among them that the ruling governments are treating them shabbily. Admittedly, their decadence does not auger well for the country for if a large minority equal to many small European, Asian and African countries remains poor, downtrodden and paralyzed, the country cannot prosper. It was perhaps in this background that the Government instituted the National Commission for Religious and Linguistic Minorities to suggest remedial measures including reservation for the weaker sections from amongst the religious and linguistic minorities. The Commission took pains in analyzing social, educational and economic conditions of minorities in details especially the conditions of Muslims vis-à-vis others. The Commission has finally recommended various welfare measures including reservation in educational institutions and government jobs in the light of various provisions of Indian Constitutions which would go a long way in transforming the fate of Indian Muslims.

The marvelous thing about Indian Constitution is that it is secular and socialistic in nature and is based on the humanistic and idealistic principles of equality, social justice and equity for all citizens irrespective of caste, creed, sex, place of birth, colour or religion. It has mandatory as well as enabling provisions for the creation of egalitarian, religion and caste neutral and exploitation free society where the privileged and the rich and famous as well as the socially, educationally and economically backward sections of the society too are equally eligible to take benefits from all policies and programmes of the Government without any fear or favour. Besides, there are several legal and constitutional provisions for safeguarding the interests of the marginalized, backward and depressed sections of the society such as SCs, STs, OBCs, weaker sections and religious and linguistic minorities to ensure their accelerated development through affirmative actions and positive discrimination to bring them at par with general category of people. Admittedly many of the rigidities and injustices of the old social structure have undergone sea change due to reservation and various special schemes and government programmes and interventions. However, there is widespread perception among the people, the civil society and the governing structure that flow of benefit to all the segments of the society has not been uniform and the poorest among them have been left out. There is a need to evolve a uniform approach and a single list of socially and economically backward classes including the religious and linguistic minorities based on common criteria so that the social justice and equality may be guaranteed to all without any discrimination.

The Wide Variety of Measures Recommended by Justice Ranganath Misra Commission

Democracy is a good form of government but it is a game of numbers where the numerically weaker sections often get marginalized by the majority. Under such circumstances the legal protection from the hegemony, dominance and preponderance of the majority community becomes a pressing need. We are lucky that to provide such a protection by law there is an Article 46 in the Directive Principle of State Policy of the Constitution which mandates the State to promote with special care the educational and economic interests of the weaker sections of the people and also to protect them from social injustice and all forms of exploitation. Keeping these factors in mind the National Commission for Religious and Linguistic Minorities headed by Justice Ranganath Misra made certain recommendations for the socially and educationally backward sections among the minorities including reservations for minorities especially the Muslims and the Neo-Buddhists. The Commission strongly felt that education was the crucial factor for social and economic advancement. It was the catalyst for improving the socio economic status of the backward sections among minorities. In the opinion of the Commission, Muslims and Buddhists were on the lower pedestal in matters of literacy merely next to SC/ST. The Census statistics revealed that the educational status of Muslims was relatively low. Muslims account for almost 65% of the total population of Muslims in Bihar, Madhya Pradesh, Rajasthan and UP but they present a dismal picture in terms of social indicators of development. Muslims have suffered from disabilities and deprivation. The National programmes like Sarva Shiksha Abhiyan have failed to educate Muslim children. The various plans adopted for the betterment of people, in general and marginalized sections, in particular have resulted in isolating socially and economically backwards of all categories since the benefits have gone to the upper crusts within the group of backwards. It is imperative that power must be vested at the lower levels from where the access to each individual, family and socially and backward section may be possible.

Based on the terms of reference, the Commission recommended a wide variety of measures for the amelioration of the Religious and Linguistic minorities. As per Term of Reference No.1 regarding the "Criteria for Identifying Socially Backward Classes among the Religious and Linguistic Minorities" the Commission suggested that the overall efforts should be directed gradually to lead the nation to a position where " the ultimate goal should be the evolution of a uniform pattern of criteria for identifying the backward, which should be based only on the educational and economic status of people and not on their caste or religion, and its application equally to all sections of the citizens irrespective of their caste or religion." The Commission, however, felt that since the achievement of the ultimate goal would take long time and require building public opinion and procuring national consensus in its favour as well as a strong political will for translating into concrete action, it suggested some other general measures to be adopted now, pending the achievement of the ultimate goal for all communities notified as minorities by executive action under National Commission for Minorities Act 1992 as well as for all religious minorities- large or small- including the Hindus in the Union Territory of Lakshadweep, and the States of Jammu & Kashmir, Meghalaya, Mizoram, Nagaland and Punjab. These measures, in its opinion, "pave the way for achieving the aforesaid stated ultimate goal in future on the one hand, while ensuring, on the other hand a faithful compliance at present with the constitutional directives of social, economic and political justice and equality of status and opportunity as proclaimed by the Preamble to the Constitution and detailed in its provisions on Fundamental rights." (16.1.1. to 16.1.4.) The Commission further recommended that "in the matter of criteria for identifying backward classes there should be absolutely no discrimination whatsoever between the majority community and the minorities, and, therefore, the criteria now applied for this purpose to the majority community - whatever that criteria may be - must be unreservedly applied also to all the minorities (16.1.5.). As a natural corollary to the aforesaid recommendation we recommend that all those classes, sections and groups among the minorities should be treated as backward whose counterparts in the majority community are regarded as backward under the present scheme of things (16.1.6.). It further recommended that all those segments within various minorities which are generally regarded as inferior within the social strata and social system of those communities should be treated as backward irrespective of the fact whether they are called 'zat' or known by any other synonymons (16.1.7.). To be more specific, we recommend that all those social and vocational groups among the minorities who but for their religious identity should have been covered by the present net of Scheduled Castes should be unquestionably treated as socially backward, irrespective of whether the religion of those other communities recognizes the caste system or not (16.1.8.). We also recommend that those groups among the minorities whose counterparts in the majority community are at present covered by the net of Scheduled Tribes should also be included in that net; and also, more specifically, members of the minority communities living in any Tribal Area from Pre-independence days should be also included irrespective of their ethnic characters (16.1.9.). The Commission recognized that the linguistic minorities might be facing some other problems like discrimination and denial of constitutional rights in practice but did not suggest any criteria for identifying the socially and economically backward classes among the linguistic minorities for it strongly felt that the concept of backwardness had no relevance for the linguistic minorities for no linguistic group may be regarded as backward by itself (16.1.10.). The Commission, however, recommended some special welfare measures without identifying language as one of the criteria for identifying backward classes for those linguistic minority groups who keep their education restricted to their own language since they are often handicapped in the matter of competing with others in respect of educational development and economic advancement (16.1.11.).

Under Term of Reference No. II, regarding measures of Welfare for Minorities including Reservation, the Commission felt that in a democracy which is the game of numbers, there was a strong possibility of the numerically weaker sections of citizens being marginalized by the majority. This is especially true of religious minorities in India where people are intensely religious and religion conscious. Under such circumstances, not only the backward sections but the minorities also need legal and constitutional protections from the hegemony and dominance of the majorities. Fortunately, Article 46, of the Directive Principle of State Policy speaks of the educational and economic interest of "weaker sections of the people" without subjecting them to backwardness. Thus, keeping this fact in mind, the Commission gave certain recommendations for the religious minorities as such as well as it recommended some special measures for the socially and educationally backward sections among minorities (16.2.1.). The Commission was of the view that the backwardness both social and economic emanated from educational backwardness and hence it recommended certain measures for educational advancement of religious minorities especially the Muslims and the Neo-Buddhists who were declared as most backward as per the national Educational Policy of 1986. At the same time, it also suggested certain measures for the economic betterment of the backward sections among the religious minorities as well as for linguistic minorities since they were entitled to certain reliefs under some specific provisions of the Constitution (16.2.2. & 16.2.3.). By the word education and its derivatives the Commission meant not only general education at the primary, secondary, graduate and postgraduate levels, but also instruction and training in engineering, technology, managerial and vocational courses and professional studies like medicine, law and accountancy. All these subjects and disciplines- as also the paraphernalia required for these like libraries, dormitories etc, were taken into consideration while recommending for the advancement of education among the minorities (16.2.4.). The Commission also strongly felt that a comprehensive law should be enacted without delay to detail all aspects of minorities' educational rights under that provision with a view to reinforcing its original dictates in letter and spirit since the "meaning and the scope of Article 30 of the Constitution has become quite uncertain, complicated and diluted due to their varied and sometimes conflicting judicial interpretations." (16.2.5.) It further recommended that "The Statute of the National Minority Educational Institutions Commission should be amended to make it wide-based in its composition, powers, functions and responsibilities and to enable it to work as the watchdog for a meticulous enforcement of all aspects of minorities'." (16.2.6.). The Commission also felt that "As by the force of judicial decisions the minority intake in minority educational institutions has, in the interest of national integration, been restricted to about 50 percent, thus virtually earmarking the remaining 50 per cent or so for the majority community- we strongly recommend that, by the same analogy and for the same purpose, at least 15 per cent seats in all non-minority educational institutions should be earmarked by law for the minorities as follows:

(a) The breakup within the recommended 15 per cent earmarked seats in institutions shall be 10 per cent for the Muslims (commensurate with their 73 per cent share of the former in the total minority population at the national level) and the remaining 5 per cent for the other minorities

(b) Minor adjustment inter se can be made in the 15 per cent earmarked seats. In the case of non-availability of Muslim candidates to fill 10 per cent earmarked seats, the remaining vacancies may be given to the other minorities if their members are available over and above their share of 5 percent; but in no case shall any seat within the recommended 15 per cent go to the majority community.

(c) As the case with Scheduled Castes and Scheduled Tribes at present, those minority community candidates who can compete with others and secure admissions on their own merit shall not be included in these 15 per cent earmarked seats. (16.2.7.)

"As regards the backward sections among all the minorities, we recommend that the concessions now available in terms of lower eligibility criteria for admission and lower rate of fee, now available to the Scheduled Casts and Scheduled tribes, should be extended also to such sections among the minorities. Since women among minorities-especially the Muslims and Buddhists - are generally educationally backward, we recommend the same measures for them as well and suggest that other possible measures be also initiated for their educational advancement." (16.2.8.)

In respect of the Muslims - who are the largest minority at the national level with a country-wide presence and yet educationally the most backward of the religious communities-we recommend certain exclusive measures as follows:

(i) Select institutions in the country like the Aligarh Muslim University and the Jamia Millia Islamia should be legally given a special responsibility to promote education at all levels to Muslim students by taking all possible steps for this purpose. At least one such institution should be selected for this purpose in each of those States and Union Territories which has a substantial Muslim population.

(ii) All schools and colleges run by the Muslims should be provided enhanced aid and other logistic facilities adequate enough to raise their standards by all possible means and maintain the same.

(iii) The Madarsa Modernization Scheme of the Government should be suitably revised, strengthened and provided with more funds so that it can provide finances and necessary paraphernalia either (a) for the provision of modern education up to Standard X within those madersas themselves which are at present imparting only religious education or, alternatively, (b) to enable the students of such madarsas to receive such education simultaneously in the general schools in their neighbourhood. The Madarsa Modernization Scheme, may for all these purpose, be operated through a central agency like the Central Wakf Council or the proposed Central Madarsa Education Board.

(iv) The rules and processes of the Central Wakf Council should be revised in such a way that its main responsibility should be educational development of the Muslims. For this purpose the Council may be legally authorized to collect a special 5 per cent educational levy from all Wakfs and to sanction utilization of Wakf lands for establishing educational institutions, polytechnics, libraries and hostels.

(v) In the funds to be distributed by the Maulana Azad Educational Foundation a suitable portion should be earmarked for the Muslims proportionate to their share in the total minority population. Out of this portion funds should be provided not only to the existing Muslim institutions but also for setting up new institutions from nursery to the highest level and for technical and vocational education anywhere in India but especially in the Muslim-concentration areas.

(vi) Anganwaris, Navodaya Vidyalayas and other similar institutions should be opened under their respective schemes especially in each of the Muslim-concentration areas and Muslim families be given suitable incentives to send their children to such institutions (16.2.9.).

For the Linguistic Minorities the Commission has recommended that:

(a) The law relating to the Linguistic Minorities Commissioner should be amended so as to make this office responsible for ensuring full implementation of all the relevant Constitutional provisions for the benefit of each such minority in all the States and Union Territories.

(b) The three-language formula should be implemented everywhere in the country making it compulsory for the authorities to include in it the mother -tongue of every child including, especially, Urdu and Punjabi and all necessary facilities, financial and logistic, should be provided by the State for education in accordance with this dispensation.

(c) Members of those linguist minority groups whose education is limited to their mother tongue and who do not have adequate knowledge of the majority language of the region should be provided special facilities in the form of scholarships, the concession and lower eligibility criteria for admission to enable them to acquire proficiency in the regionally dominant language.

(d) Urdu-medium schools should be provided special aid and assistance - financial and otherwise-to enhance and improve their efficiency, standards and results.

Under Term of Reference No. 1, pertaining to criteria for Identifying Socially Backward Classes among the Religious and Linguistic Minorities, the Commission felt that the ultimate criteria in the long run should be based only on the educational and economic status of people and not on caste and religion. However, till the evolution of the said goal, the Commission recommended the criteria applied for majority community must be necessarily applied to all the minorities without any kind of discrimination. All those classes, sections and groups in minorities too should be treated as backward whose counterparts in the majority community are regarded as backward including those who are generally considered as " "inferior" within the social strata and social system of those communities. Moreover, the Commission also felt that all those social and vocational groups among minorities who but for their religion could not be covered under the net of Scheduled Castes should be treated as socially backward whether the religion of those communities recognize caste system or not. Similarly, all those groups in the minorities whose counterparts in the majority community have been brought within the purview of Scheduled Tribes should also be brought in that net including members of the minority group living in tribal area from pre-independence irrespective of their ethnic nature. The Commission did not recommend any criteria for identifying the socially and economically backward classes among the Linguistic Minorities for it found no relevance of backwardness with linguistic minorities. However, it recommended some specific welfare measures for those linguistic minority groups who keep their education restricted to their own language since their wards are often handicapped in matter of competing with others. The Commission feared that the numerically weaker sections in a democracy especially the Religious

Minorities tended to be marginalized by the hegemony and preponderance of the religion conscious majority community and hence the religious minorities as a whole and not just that of the backward sections among them need legal and constitutional protection. Keeping Article 46 of the Directive Principle of State Policy in mind the Commission made certain recommendations for the religious minorities though it also suggested some special measures for socially and educationally backward sections among the minorities.

The Salient Features of Misra Commission

The conviction of the Commission that backwardness- both social and economic actually emanates from educational backwardness speaks volumes of the genius and far-sightedness of the members constituting the Commission. They have aptly emphasized on the role of education for the growth and development of Minorities especially the Muslims and Neo-Buddhists. The quality of human capital as well as its augmentation not only augment democratic participation, upgrade health and quality of life but also facilitate social and economic progress of the depressed and marginalized sections of the society. Opening up of the doors of educational institutions for weaker sections of the society through affirmative actions enhance efficiency, open up opportunities and augment earnings. If we look at the broad perspective on issues relating to the education of Muslims in India we find that Muslims suffer both from the low level as well as low quality of education. Their deprivation in matters of education increases as the quality and level of education rise. Besides, with the accelerated development of educational institutions in the country, not only Muslims are lagging behind, but the educational deficit between them and others is increasing. It is irony of fate that in the colourful conglomeration of numerous races, religions, sects, cultures and traditions Muslims find them neglected, depressed and alone. Thus, a significant policy shift recommended by the Commission in recognizing the problem of educational depravity among Muslims and in devising corrective measures as well as in allocating resources for their development in meaningful time horizon would go a long way in integrating them in the national mainstream.

The beauty of the approach of the Commission is that while recommending corrective measures for educational development, it covered education from nursery to super-specialties including engineering, technology, medicine, accountancy, managerial and professional courses and also suggested a suitable support system including libraries, reading rooms, laboratories, hostels and dormitories etc. It also recommended for the enactment of a comprehensive law to reinforce the spirit of Article 30 which has been distorted by several legal and administrative interpretations. It has also felt the need for the amendment of the statute of the National Minority Educational Institution Commission to enable it to work as watchdog for educational rights of minorities under the Constitution. Besides, since the 50 per cent seats in the minority institutions are meant for majority community, the Commission has boldly suggested 10 per cent seats for Muslims in the entire majority run educational institutions. It has also suggested that the minority community candidates who secure admission on the basis of their open merit be excluded from 15 per cent earmarked seats on the pattern of Scheduled Caste and Scheduled Tribe students. Moreover, for backward sections among minorities especially the women candidates from Muslims and Neo-Buddhist, the Commission has suggested concessions in matters of eligibility, lower fee and other benefits at par with Scheduled Castes and Scheduled Tribes. Muslims of India are demanding Minority character for Aligarh Muslim University and Jamia Millia Islamia with a view to openly, legally and transparently benefit Muslim students but they have failed to get such rights from Indian Parliament till date due to various legal, judicial and political hurdles. Thanks to the Commission that it has felt the need to provide legally the special responsibilities and powers to select institutions in the country such as Aligarh Muslim University and Jamia Millia Islamia so that they may promote education of Muslims at all levels. Not only this, it has also recommended that at least one such institution should be selected for this purpose in each of those States and Union Territories which has substantial Muslim population. Moreover, its recommendations for providing enhanced aids and logistic support to schools and colleges run by Muslims are praiseworthy. Its suggestions to grant greater funds and necessary paraphernalia to Madarsa Modernization Scheme for providing modern education or facilitating the Madarsa students to move to mainstream and revising the rules of Central Wakf Council so that it may legally collect special 5 per cent educational levy from all Wakfs for establishing polytechnics, libraries, hostels and educational institutions are worth consideration. Likewise, the distribution of a suitable quantity of financial resources and funds commensurate to the share of Muslims in total minority population by the Maulana Azad Educational Foundation to the existing and the new institutions from nursery to the highest levels is the need of the hour. Similarly, the opening of Anganwaris, Navodaya Vidyalayas and similar institutions in Muslim-concentration areas along with incentives to Muslim families to send their children in such institutes posses great potential to enhance education to Muslim children at grass root level. Muslims are very bitter for neglecting the Urdu schools and showing the step-brotherly treatment to Urdu and not teaching in their mother-tongue at primary level despite the existence of the three-language formula. The Commission has rightly felt the need of amending the law relating to the Linguistic Minorities Commissioner for ensuring full protection of Constitutional provisions for the benefit of each minority as well as for the implementation of three-language formula making it compulsory to include in it the mother-tongue of the child including specially the Urdu and Punjabi. It has also recommended special aid and assistance to Urdu-medium schools and scholarships, fee concessions and lower eligibility criteria to those students whose education is limited to their mother tongue and who do not have adequate knowledge of majority language so that they may acquire proficiency in the regionally dominant language.

On the economic front the Commission felt that several minority groups especially among Muslims were engaged in household and small scale industries and hence there was an urgent need to modernize such industries as well as to provide training to artisans and workmen in these areas (16.2.11.). Besides, since Muslims as well as some other minorities have scant or weak presence in agrarian sector, there is need to formulate schemes for the development of agriculture, agronomy and agricultural trade among them (16.2.12). The Commission also suggested the promotion and popularization of self-employment and income generation schemes among the minorities with a view to augment their financial resources (16.2.13). The Commission also recommended that the rules, regulation and processes of the National Minorities Development and Finance Corporation be overhauled on priority basis in the light of the report submitted by the NMDFC in order to make it more efficient, effective and far-reaching among minorities (16.2.14). The Commission further recommended that "a 15 per cent share be earmarked for the minorities- with a break-up of 10 per cent for the Muslims (commensurate with their 73 per cent share of the former in the total minority population at the national level) - and 5 per cent for the other minorities in all government schemes like Rural Employment Generation Programme, Prime Minister's Rozgar Yojna, Grameen Yojna, etc.(16.2.15). The Commission further stressed that "Since the minorities-especially the Muslims-are very much under-represented, and sometimes wholly unrepresented, in government employment, we recommend that they should be regarded as backward in this respect within the meaning of that term as used in Article 16(4) of the Constitution- notably without qualifying the word "backward" with the words "socially and educationally" and that 15 per cent of all posts in all cadres and grades under the Central and State Government should be earmarked for them as follows:

(a) The break up within the recommended 15 per cent shall be 10 per cent for the Muslims (commensurate with their 73 per cent share of the former in the total minority population at the national level) and the remaining 5 per cent for other minorities.

(b) Minor adjustment inter se can be made within the 15 per cent earmarked seats. In the case of non-availability of Muslims to fill 10 per cent earmarked seats, the remaining vacancies may be given to other minorities if their numbers are available over and above of 5 percent; but in no case shall any seat within the recommended 15 per cent go to the majority community (16.2.16). The Commission maintained that "We are convinced that the action recommended by us above will have full sanction of Article 16(4) of the Constitution. Yet, should there be some insurmountable difficulty in implementing this recommendation, as an alternative we recommend that since according to the Mandal Commission Report the minorities constitute 8.4 per cent of the total OBC quota, in the 27 per cent OBC quota and 8.4 per cent sub-quota should be earmarked for the minorities with an internal break-up of 6 per cent for the Muslims (commensurate with their 73 per cent share in the total minority population at the national level) and 2.4 per cent share in the total minority population for other minorities-with minor adjustments inter se in accordance with population of various minorities in various States and UTs (16.2.17). The Commission further recommended that the reservation now extended to the Scheduled Tribes, which is a religion-neutral class, should be carefully examined to assess the extent of minority presence in it and remedial measures should be initiated to correct the imbalance, if any. The situation in Meghalaya, Mizoram, Nagaland and Lakshadweep which are minority-dominated and predominantly tribal, as also such tribal areas/districts in Assam and other States, is to be especially taken into account in this respect. (16.2.18). Finally the Commission recommended that the judicial reservation recently expressed in several cases about the continued inclusion of the creamy layer in various classes enjoying reservation, inclusive of the Scheduled Castes and Scheduled Tribes, should be seriously considered for acceptance as a State Policy (16.2.17).

Commission's Views Regarding the Additional Term of Reference

Regarding the Additional Term of Reference pertaining to Para 3 of the Constitution(Scheduled Castes) Order 1950, added by the Government to the original Terms of Reference, the Commission felt that "caste is in fact a social phenomenon shared by almost all Indian communities irrespective of their religious persuasions. Many of the particular castes are found simultaneously in various religious communities, equally facing problems of social degradation and mistreatment both by their co-religionists and the others.(16.3.1) The Commission further stressed that "the Constitution of India prohibits any discrimination between the citizens on the basis of caste, and yet it sanctions special affirmative measures for Scheduled Castes. At the same time it prohibits any discrimination on the ground of religion. Reading all these constitutional provisions together, we are convinced that any religion-based discrimination in selecting particular castes for affirmative action will conflict with the letter and spirit of the constitutional provisions. (16.3.2.) The Commission recommended that "the caste system should be recognized as a general social characteristic of the Indian society as a whole, without questioning whether the philosophy and teachings of any particular religion recognize it or not- since the Indian brands of certain faith traditions like Christianity and Islam have never assimilated many puritan principles of those religions, posing this question in respect of the caste system only and singling out for a differential treatment is unreasonable and unrealistic. (16.3.3.) The Commission further stressed that "We would like this fact to be duly recognized that among the Muslims of India the concepts of *Zat* (caste) and *arzal* (lower castes) are very much in practice; and even the Muslim law of marriage recognizes the doctrine of *kufw*-parity in marriage between the parties in all vital aspects including social status and descent- which in this country means nothing but caste." (16.3.4.) In view of the above fact the Commission recommended that "Para 3 of the Constitution (Scheduled Castes) Order 1950- which originally restricted the Scheduled Caste net to the Hindus and later opened it to Sikhs and Buddhists, thus still excluding from its purview the Muslims, Christians, Jains and Parsis etc. - should be wholly deleted by appropriate action so as to completely de-link the Scheduled Caste status from religion and make the Scheduled Castes net fully religion-neutral like that of the Scheduled Tribes." (16.3.5.) The Commission further recommended "that all those groups and classes among the Muslims and Christians, etc., whose counterparts among the Hindus, Sikhs or Buddhists, are included in the Central or State Scheduled Castes lists should also be covered by the Scheduled Caste net. If any such group or class among the Muslims and Christians, etc., is now included in an OBC list, it should be deleted from their while transferring it to the Scheduled Castes-placing the same persons in the Scheduled Caste list if they are Hindu, Sikh or Buddhist but in the OBC list if they follow any other religion-which is the case in many States - in our opinion clearly amounts to religion-based discrimination." (16.3.6.) The Commission finally concluded that "as the Constitution of India guarantees freedom of conscience and religious freedom as a Fundamental Right, once a person has been included in a Scheduled Caste list a willful change of religion on his part should not affect adversely his or her Scheduled Caste status-as that would in our opinion conflict with the basic constitutional provisions relating to equity, justice and non-discrimination on religious grounds; as also with the spirit of the old and time-tested Caste Disabilities Removal Act of 1850. (16.3.7.)

Incidentally, the Member-Secretary of the Commission submitted the last minute dissent note to the Commission highlighting the following facts:

"(i) There is no justification for inclusion of SC converts to Christianity or SC converts to Islam as Scheduled Castes.

(ii) The Constitution (SC) Order 1950 issued under Article 341 of the Constitution read with Article 15(4) is religion based. Therefore, the condition of 'religion' from Para 3 of the order should not be deleted.

(iii) The ceiling of 50 per cent of reservation should continue as has been adjudicated by the Supreme Court.

(iv) As SC converts to Christianity/Islam do not qualify for inclusion as SCs and avail of facilities and reservations given to the OBCs until a comprehensive list of SRB's is prepared." (Page 168 of the Report of the Commission) The Member -Secretary strongly felt that before coming to any conclusion historical, constitutional and legal position should thoroughly be examined since the basis of identification of a certain class of people as Scheduled Caste was social, educational and economic backwardness arising from the age-old traditional practice of untouchability that was an inseparable concomitant of Hindu religion. The Scheduled Caste status to Sikh and Buddhist was given because they were basically the sects of Hindu religion rather than being independent religions like Christianity or Islam. Besides, Christianity or Islam were not treated as Depressed Class/Scheduled caste by British in pre-Independent India as well as by the Indian Government after independence. It was also stressed that persons of Scheduled Caste origin converted to Christianity or Islam who were educationally backward were included in the list of OBC and were getting several benefits from schemes and institutional support system formulated for OBCs including reservation in educational institutions as well as in government services. Apart from the above favours they are getting benefits from constitutional, legal and institutional protection as members of minority communities. Lastly, it was stated that SCs and STs were accorded reservation to the extent of 15% and 7.5% respectively despite the fact that their share in population as per 2001 Census was on the higher side. Thus, the Member-Secretary concluded that the grant of SC status to the converts to Christianity or Islam would adversely affect the benefits available to SCs in matters of education, services and the related matters.

The Chairman Justice RN' Misra and Members Dr. Anil Wilson and Dr. Mohinder Singh fully endorsed the views expressed by NCRLM Member Dr. Tahir Mahmood emphasizing that there was no indication whatsoever in the Constitution-either in Article 341 or elsewhere - of an intention that Scheduled Castes must remain confined to any particular religion or religions. Such a link was unwarrantedly created by the executive action while issuing the Constitution (Scheduled Castes) Order 1950. They also refuted the contention that Article 25 of the Constitution supported the view that Sikh, Buddhist and Jain faiths were to be regarded as off-shoots of Hindu religion. If it is accepted for argument sake that Sikh, Buddhist and Jain faiths were integral part of Hinduism, why did the Constitution (Scheduled Castes) Order 1950 initially declare that no non-Hindu could be a Scheduled

Caste? Besides, why it took the Sikhs six years and the Buddhists another 14 years to get themselves included in the Scheduled Caste net? Why Jains are even now excluded from it? It appears that originally the Scheduled Castes status was conferred only upon Hindus for some supra-Constitutional reasons and later on as an afterthought the net was extended to Sikhs and Buddhists erroneously seeking support from the Constitution. It was also emphasized that the dissent note wrongly asserted that Sikh and Buddhist religions were not independent religions but home grown sects within Hindu religion when the fact is that Sikhs and Buddhists always regarded their religions as independent ones. Moreover, it was un-constitutional as well as unwise to create distinctions between two types of artificially created categories of home grown religions and those originated outside India. Over and above this, Para 3 conflicts with the Constitutional guarantees of equality of status and opportunity since the serious drawback of Constitution(SC) Order 1950 is that despite being born in the same caste listed as Scheduled Caste one cannot be included in the net of Scheduled Castes because one is not Hindu, Sikh or Buddhist. The above Members of the Commission including the Chairman thus unanimously recommended the repeal of Para 3 of the Constitution (Scheduled Castes) Order 1950 considering it wholly repugnant to the letter and spirit of the Constitution.

Modalities to Implement Commissions Welfare Measures

As per Term of Reference No. III pertaining to Modalities, the Commission was asked to suggest the necessary constitutional, legal and administrative modalities needed to implement the recommendations. (16.4.1.) The Commission, however, did not suggest any amendment in the Constitution as none of their recommendations needed any amendment in the Constitution since each of them could be implemented by legislative or administrative action. (16.4.2.) The Commission recommended for the suitable amendment of all Central and State Acts, Statutory Rules and Regulations which in the opinion of the Ministry of Law and Justice or any other concerned authority required such amendments for the implementation of the recommendations of the Commission. (16.4.3.)

Legislative Actions Recommended

The Commission recommended the following legislative actions since they were not only needed for the implementation of some of their recommendations but were in the interest of the minorities.

"(a) Enactment of a detailed law to enforce the dictates of Article 30 of the Constitution;

(b) Amendment of the National Commission for Backward Classes Act 1993;

(c) Amendment of the Constitution (Scheduled Castes) Order 1950 and the Constitution (Scheduled Tribes) Order 1951 as also the Central and State lists of the Scheduled Castes and Scheduled Tribes;

(d) Review of the laws and rules, processes and procedures, relating to selection and notification of OBCs at the Central and State levels;

(e) Enactment of law to clothe with statutory status and judicial enforceability the Prime Minister's 15-Point Programme for Minorities 1983 as modified in 2006.

(f) The Commission also suggested for the amendment of the National Commission for Minorities Act 1992 and the National Commission for Educational Institutions Act 2004 with a view to appoint reputed experts in the constitutional, legal, educational and economic fields through a search committee as in the case of National Human Rights Commission.

(g) The Commission also recommended "necessary amendments in the Wakf Act 1993 as well as all the Rules framed under its provisions; and also

(h) Review and necessary overhaul of the laws, rules, regulations, procedures and processes relating to the National Minorities Development and Finance Corporations and the Maulana Azad Education Foundation." (16.4.4)

The Commission also recommended the following administrative measures as they were needed for the implementation of some of their recommendations as well as they were beneficial for Minorities.

Administrative Measures Recommended

(a) "Establishment of a Parliamentary Committee to consider and decide in the light of the Constitution policy matters relating to the minorities;

(b) Establishment of a National Committee consisting of Chairpersons of NHRC, NCW, NCBC, NCST, NCSC, NCM, NCMEI, NMDFC, CLM, Central Wakf Council and Maulana Azad Foundation along with nominated experts for monitoring the educational and economic development of the minorities;

(c) Creation of similar bodies in all the States/UTs for the same purpose and consisting of local top-level officials dealing with minority related matters and independent experts;

(d) Establishment of a National-level Coordination Committee consisting of representative of all the nationalized banks and other financial institutions to work under the RBI for monitoring credit flow to the minorities;

(e) Establishment of State Minorities Commissions and Minority Welfare Departments in all those States and UTs where these do not exist as of now:

(f) Decentralization of all minority related schemes, programs and plans so as to create suitable district-level mechanisms for their day-to-day implementation;

(g) Revision of the list of the Minority Concentration Districts as suggested by the NCM in 1990s and initiating special educational, economic and general welfare measures there through the local administration;

(h) Appointment of Minority Welfare Committee consisting of officials and local experts in all districts of the country to act as the nodal agencies of NCM, State Minorities Commissions and all other Central and State-level bodies working for the minorities." (16.4.5.)

General Consensus Among Muslims in Favour of Reservation

The Commission has certainly done a great service to the nation, in general and Indian Minorities, in particular by intelligently analyzing their problems and boldly suggesting reservation for them in educational institutions and government services. It has brilliantly suggested several welfare measures for the weaker sections of the society and beautifully chalked out the modalities for the implementation of its recommendations by recommending several concrete measures but the irony of fate is that Muslims are very skeptical and apprehensive about such Committees and Commissions of the Government. They consider them as the beautiful political moves by the players in the hierarchy of governing structure to placate the Minorities without doing anything substantial for them. There was much trepidation and skepticism regarding the setting up of Sachar Committee. Many welcomed the move but there were several sensible people who considered it as a ploy by the Government to divert the attention of the people from failures on the part of the Government in matters of empowerment of Muslims. There is a sense of despair and dejection among Muslims even after the publication of the said Report for there appears to be lack of strong will on the part of the Government to implement the recommendations of the Sachar Committee Report in letter and spirit. Muslims are bitter of approaching the Government and presenting their demands to redress their grievances. They have lost all hopes in what the Government professes and says about them. They want results. The non-implementation of various earlier Commissions and Committees have made them wary of any new initiative. Unless and until there is a fundamental change in the mindset of the Government and substantial transformation in the perception of the civil society, the reports of the commissions and committees would be placed under the debris. Many difficulties arise at the implementation stage because Muslims, problems are treated merely as the problems of a minority in the context of the partition of the country and not as a national concern.

Muslims' perceptions have not been built in air. They have seen the fate of the recommendations of many Commissions and Committees including the end result of Sachar Committee Report. They fear that in the absence of the lack of strong will on the part of the ruling Government at the Centre, it would be difficult to implement the recommendations of the Misra Commission holistically. They know it for sure that the

Backward Classes would resist any reduction in their 27 per cent quota so also the Scheduled Castes and the Scheduled Tribes would oppose tooth and nail any encroachment in their 22.5 per cent allocation. Similarly, the Higher Castes would not lag behind. They too will not allow the government to cross the 50 per cent limit imposed by the Supreme Court. Besides, many NGOs would run towards courts to scuttle reservation for Muslims on the basis of religion. Over and above this, the right wing extremist parties would never digest the idea that, any concession is given to Muslims in matters of education and employment. In the wake of coalition and vote-bank politics where no single party has absolute majority, the recommendations of the Commission would generate more heat than light. Just as the right wing parties told to their followers that give us absolute majority in the Parliament and State Assemblies and we would give you Ram Mandir at the sight of Babri Masjid. Similarly, the secular parties would say the same thing to the Muslims in lieu of reservation in educational institutions and government jobs. In this quid pro quo, Muslims would always remain losers due to their weak numerical strength and historical past.

Lastly, we would like to conclude by emphasizing that the Commission rightly recommended reservation for Muslims in educational institutions considering them educationally most backward and justified it by saying that backwardness, both social and economic, emanated from educational backwardness. Similarly, it appropriately suggested reservation in Government jobs by supporting that Muslims being one of the largest minorities of the country were under-represented and sometimes wholly un-represented in Government jobs which did not auger well for the health of the country. The Commission knew it fully well that Muslims despite being a significant part of the electorate were grossly under-represented in the Parliament, State Assemblies and grass root institutions for they were scattered and could not get elected by themselves due to their weak numerical strength in the democracy which was the game of numbers. It appears that as per Terms of Reference No. II pertaining to measures of welfare for minorities including reservation, the Commission could not recommend reservation for minorities especially

Muslims in legislative and other grass root institutions, because, in the said terms of reference, the reservation was confined to the field of education and government employment only. It appears that either the Government wants to go slow or it could not muster courage to think of giving reservation to Muslims in the legislative bodies at this stage due to the fear of opposition from the right wing and interested parties. However, the fact is that it is the need of the hour. Muslims of India are suffocating due to the lack of voice in the governing structure. They strongly feel that Muslims' political participation at the national level as well as State level, local self government bodies and grassroots institutions is essential to achieve equity. They complain that they are non-entities in political sphere because there is no space for them in the country's power group. They are systematically denied political participation through various devices. Many a time their names are not included in the voters' list and sometimes Muslim concentration areas are declared as reserved. Moreover, Muslims have to depend upon the majority community to get elected as they are spread throughout the country and there are very few constituencies from where they may be declared elected on their own strength. Unfortunately due to manipulation of votes on communal lines at the last minute the balance is tilted against them. It is because of this reason that Muslim's representation is the lowest in both the Houses of Parliament as well as State Assemblies. Instead of around 100 Members in Lok Sabha and about 50 Members in Rajya Sabha on the bases of Muslims share in total population, hardly 50 to 60 Members reach both the Houses from various political parties which make them weak and irrelevant. Presently, Muslims are negligible in Parliament, State Assemblies, Zila Parishads and Panchayats. There are very few Ministers, Zila Pramukhs and Pradhans among Muslims because of which they fail to get various benefits from the political structure of the country. Due to lack of political voice, the number of governors, chairmen of various bodies, Committees and Commissions too are meager among Muslims. Since there is no reservation for them at grass root levels, they fail to get various benefits provided by Panchayats, Municipal Corporations and District level bodies such as roads, houses, sanitation, cheap loans and surplus lands etc. As against this, the Scheduled Castes and Scheduled Tribes have a dominant voice at national, states as well as grass root levels and no one can dare to challenge them. Consequently, many benefits have flown to them which have made them prosperous.

It is, therefore, necessary that in matters of reservation there should be no discrimination whatsoever between the majority community and the minorities at the levels of Parliament, State Assemblies and grass root institutions. The criteria now applied to Scheduled Castes and Scheduled Tribes based on their socio-economic backwardness must also be unreservedly applied to Muslims who have come to the stage of Scheduled Castes during the last sixty years. We have aptly demonstrated in the previous chapters that Muslims as a whole both at the national level and at the level of States are more backward socially, economically and educationally compared to general Hindus, Hindu Upper Castes, Hindu OBCs, other minorities and even Hindu Scheduled Castes and Scheduled Tribes in many segments. Since they have been drifted in the debris of decadence, at least 15 per cent seats in Parliament, State Assemblies and grass root levels should be earmarked for the minorities on the pattern of Scheduled Castes and Scheduled Tribes- with breakup of 10 per cent for the Muslims (commensurate with their population share in total minority population) and 5 per cent for other backward minorities with the condition that in case of non-availability of Muslim candidates the surplus seats may be given only to other minorities and in no case to the majority candidates. Needless to say that the addition of merely 70 to 80 seats for Muslims and 20 to 25 to other Minorities in the Parliament would not make much difference in the composition of the Parliament or State Assemblies. On the contrary, the relatively larger number of minorities would make the Parliament and Assemblies more colourful and meaningful. Besides, all other concessions now available to Scheduled Castes and Scheduled Tribes in matters of eligibility criteria, granting loans, housing and other facilities should also apply to backward minorities including Muslims. The Indian Constitution is committed to the equality of citizens irrespective of their castes, class, creed, sex, religion or place of birth. Winning the confidence of the Minorities and meeting their aspirations and ensuring their rights not only enhance the dignity and equality of the backward segments of the society but also contribute to the political and social stability and help in lessening the tensions, dissensions and frictions among the groups and individuals in the country. India is a colourful rainbow of various races, religions, sects, cultures and traditions and it has been ensured in the Constitution that the color of minorities would not be allowed to become dim at any cost. Besides, every just and civilized state is presumed to preserve, protect and promote the rights, heritage and identities of minorities in an impartial and compassionate manner.

There is no doubt in it that what we have stated about the deplorable profile of Muslims is an eye opener for the Central and the State Governments as well as the large sections of the civil society as well as the well-wishers of Muslims. The facts and figures convincingly lead to the conclusion that the affirmative and the positive steps are highly essential to salvage the pathetic problems of Muslims. If they are left to chance or at the hands of competitive forces, the merciless global competition and the Laissez fare would reduce them to the status of second or third class citizens. We have also analyzed the recommendations in much details in the hope that they would receive the attention of the respective Governments and the general society as well as the people of India and the said recommendations would not be thrown in the debris but would be implemented with all earnestness and urgency they deserve. It was also emphasized time and again that the implementation of the Misra Commission report would not only benefit Muslim community but it would also enhance India's prestige as a secular democracy and reflect upon the large-hearted tolerance of the majority community and would go a long way in enriching the age-old pluralistic culture of the country. Now the ball is in the court of the ruling government. Let us see how it plays with it.

References

The facts and figures in the book have been mostly drawn from Sachar Committee Report and the findings of the National Commission for Religious and Linguistic Minorities. The author has quoted the sources at the proper places in the book which may by verified for further research from the following material.

A Report prepared by the Prime Minister's High Level Committee under the Chairmanship of Justice Rajendar Sachar entitled "Social, Economic and Educational Status of the Muslim Community of India" November 2006, p. 403, sections 12, Tables 11.2 and Appendix Tables 10.4, including references, Technical Notes, Appendix and Commissioned Papers.

The Report prepared by the Ministry of Minority Affair's High power Committee under the Chairmanship of Justice Ranganth Misra entitled "National Commission for Religious and Linguistic Minorities" May 2007. It is spread over two volumes.

Volume I contains 188 p., 10 Chapters and 7 Appendices and 76 Tables.

Volume II contains 8 Annexures, 51 Sub Annexures and 224 p.

Index